W9-BJD-233

AROUND

paris
WITH KIDS

2nd Edition

by Emily Emerson

Fodor's Travel Publications
New York • Toronto • London • Sydney • Auckland

www.fodors.com

CREDITS
Writer: Emily Emerson

Series Editors: Karen Cure, Andrea Lehman
Editor: Linda Cabasin
Editorial Production: Tom Holton
Production/Manufacturing: Robert Shields

Design: Fabrizio La Rocca, *creative director*; Tigist Getachew, *art director*
Illustration and Series Design: Rico Lins, Keren Ora Admoni/Rico Lins Studio

ABOUT THE WRITER

Emily Emerson is an American writer who moved to France for a year in 1979 and can't seem to leave. These days she and her 12-year-old daughter, Ghislaine, divide their time between Paris and their ramshackle 15th-century farmhouse in the Loire Valley.

Fodor's Around Paris with Kids

Copyright © 2003 by Fodors LLC

Fodor's is a registered trademark of Random House, Inc. All rights reserved under International and Pan-American Copyright Conventions. Published in the United States by Fodor's Travel Publications, a unit of Fodors LLC, a subsidiary of Random House, Inc., and simultaneously in Canada by Random House of Canada Limited, Toronto. Distributed by Random House, Inc., New York.

Second Edition
ISBN 1-4000-1150-7
ISSN 1533-5313

Important Tip
Although all prices, opening times, and other details in this book are based on information supplied to us at press time, changes occur all the time in the travel world, and Fodor's cannot accept responsibility for facts that become outdated or for inadvertent errors or omissions. So always confirm information when it matters, especially if you're making a detour to visit a specific place.

Special Sales
Fodor's Travel Publications are available at special discounts for bulk purchases for sales promotions or premiums. Special editions, including personalized covers, excerpts of existing guides, and corporate imprints, can be created in large quantities for special needs. For more information, contact your local bookseller or Special Markets, Fodor's Travel Publications, 1745 Broadway, New York, NY 10019. Inquiries from Canada should be directed to your local Canadian bookseller or sent to Random House of Canada, Ltd., Marketing Dept., 2775 Matheson Boulevard East, Mississauga, Ontario L4W 4P7. Inquiries from the United Kingdom should be sent to Fodor's Travel Publications, 20 Vauxhall Bridge Road, London, England SW1V 2SA.

PRINTED IN THE UNITED STATES OF AMERICA
10 9 8 7 6 5 4 3 2 1

COUNTDOWN TO GOOD TIMES

GET READY, GET SET!

Paris may be the world's most romantic capital, but it's also a great place to visit with kids, even if you don't speak French. What you'll find in this book are 68 ways to have a terrific couple of hours or an entire day with children in tow. I've scoured the city, digging out things your kids—and you—will love, from the state-of-the-art kids' museum in the La Villette complex to a close-up view of gargoyles from the roof of Notre-Dame. Almost anywhere you go in Paris, you'll find pretty little parks, tasty snacks, and kid-friendly attractions, because this sophisticated city has made a big effort to develop a wealth of educational and fun activities for young Parisians and visitors.

My advice is to head first for the Eiffel Tower, hands-down the city's top sight for most kids, and then to relax in the Jardin du Luxembourg, a very Parisian park with something for everyone. Another big hit, especially at night, is a ride on one of the *bateaux mouches* tour boats that cruise the Seine. Use the neighborhood directory (All Around Town) and the thematic directory (Something for Everyone) at the back of this book to help make your plans. Whatever you do, avoid museum overload and take the time to sit on a park bench, munch a baguette and a piece of cheese, and remind yourself you're really, truly in Paris.

SAVING MONEY

Only regular adult and kids' prices are listed; children under the ages specified are free. Always ask whether any discounts are offered for a particular status or affiliation (bring your I.D.). Many attractions sell family tickets or long-term memberships. Some places—mostly museums and other cultural destinations—have free admission one day a month (usually Sunday) or one day a week after a certain time.

The invaluable Carte Musées et Monuments (available at participating museums and monuments, tourist offices, métro stations and FNAC stores; see www.intermusees.com) gets you into 70 local museums and monuments at a discount and often without standing in line; one-day (€15), three-day (€30) or five-day (€45) cards are available. You can also purchase special transportation-plus-admission tickets for many attractions just outside Paris.

The Carte Orange, with unlimited métro and bus travel for a month, can be a big money-saver; choose your card by the number of zones. A two-zone card covers central Paris and the near suburbs, and kids' cards are available at a discount. The Paris-Visite card, sold at all métro and train stations, furnishes unlimited travel on area métros, trains, and buses for one to five days; passes for kids 4–11 are half price. This card also grants discounts to a number of attractions.

EATING OUT

Paris restaurants are generally more expensive than their U.S. counterparts, but most offer kids' menus or will prepare a special kids' meal on request. Yes, you can find kids' hamburgers and steaks (specify *bien cuit* if you don't want them served rare) and *frites* (french fries), but French-style fast food is more likely to consist of crêpes (look for street-corner stands everywhere), croque monsieur sandwiches (grilled ham and cheese), and baguette sandwiches. Other on-the-go options can be picked up at charcuteries (takeout meat and food shops) and pâtisseries (pastry shops). Picnickers should note that most city parks don't let you sit on the grass (though it's generally fine to do so in the city's *bois*, or woods). Do what the French do, and have your picnic on a park bench.

Many Paris restaurants close in August, and most close at least one day a week, usually Sunday or Monday. Call ahead to make sure a restaurant will be open and to make reservations. Lunch is generally served from 11:30 to 3, and the evening meal begins at around 7:30. Tearooms, brasseries, and cafés tend to be open during the day, though tearooms often close in the evening. Café prices are cheaper if you sit at the counter, but you'll be surrounded by smokers. Though Paris restaurants must provide nonsmoking sections (*zones non-fumeur*), these are usually small and are never at the counter or bar. Restaurants serving American cuisine tend to have larger nonsmoking sections, and organic or vegetarian restaurants tend to attract few smokers.

GETTING AROUND
Paris is divided into 20 arrondissements (administrative districts), each with its own character and its own *mairie* (city hall). Arrondissements are listed in the French manner (e.g., 6e is the 6th arrondissement), following addresses.

Traffic is heavy throughout Paris, sidewalks are small and crowded, and people drive really, really fast. Be especially careful crossing streets; many drivers run red lights. Skaters and even scooter-riders often take shortcuts on sidewalks. On the métro, watch for the gap between platforms and cars, and hold children's hands when boarding.

The Paris métro system is fast, efficient, economical, and generally safe, although you should avoid empty cars at night and watch out for pickpockets; the métro closes at around 1 AM. One ticket per person lets you ride as far as you like within central Paris. Kids' tickets are discounted. A 10-ticket *carnet* is more economical than buying separate tickets; a Carte Orange (*see* Saving Money, *above*) is the best choice if you're planning a long stay. The RER system (suburban commuter trains, such as the ones that run to the two Paris airports) requires separate RER tickets, available from ticket booths in RER stations. Paris buses are fun for kids, but the routes are sometimes difficult to follow. (Pick up a "Paris Bus" brochure at any métro station.) You can pay with a métro ticket or cash, but each time you change buses, you must pay again.

WHEN TO GO
With the exception of seasonal attractions, kid-oriented destinations are generally busiest when children are out of school—especially weekends, Wednesdays (when many French schools either organize field trips or have no classes), holidays (especially two-week school vacations in mid-February, at Easter, and in mid-November), and July and August. Most sights are less crowded at meal times (1–2 and 7–9). Some attractions are closed when schools are closed, but others add extra hours on these days. Check ahead if you want to see an attraction on a holiday.

RESOURCES AND INFORMATION
If you have special interests or want to find out about events scheduled during your visit, contact the Office de Tourisme de la Ville de Paris (127 av. Champs-Elysées, tel. 08–92–68–31–12, www.parisbienvenue.com) or the Espace du Tourisme d'Ile de France (Carrousel du Louvre underground shopping mall, 99 rue de Rivoli, tel. 01–44–50–19–98). The Web site of the Mairie de Paris (www.paris-france.org) is another good source.

Check out the free, English-language publications *Paris Voice* (www.parisvoice.com) and *FUSAC (France-USA Contacts*, www.fusac.com), available at W.H. Smith bookstore (rue de Rivoli) and other locations. For information (in French) on weekly events, try *Pariscope* (www.pariscope.fr), *Time Out* (www.timeout.com/paris), *Le Monde* (www.lemonde.fr), and *Libération* (www.liberation.fr), available at newsstands. The Web site www.gratuitpourlesenfants.com covers free activities for kids in France. *Paris-Mômes,* an excellent, free bi-monthly supplement describing events just for kids, appears in *Libération* newspaper and is distributed in various shops and museums. If your kids would like to practice French on a French Web site for kids, try www.momes.net.

FINAL THOUGHTS

Lots of moms and dads were interviewed to create these suggestions, and we'd love to add yours. E-mail us at editors@fodors.com (specify Around Paris with Kids on the subject line), or write to us at Fodor's Around Paris with Kids, 1745 Broadway, 14th floor, New York, NY 10019. In the meantime, bon voyage!

—Emily Emerson

AQUABOULEVARD

Paris may be in northern Europe, but you'd never know it once you step into this water-lovers' wonderland. A year-round indoor-outdoor water park, Aquaboulevard lets you take a trip to the tropics without leaving the heart of the city. In summer, Aquaboulevard's outdoor beach and pool area, open June–August, is one of the city's most popular sunbathing spots.

Feel like basking on the sand? You can, on the artificial beach surrounding the outdoor pool. Want to bodysurf? The waves won't please experienced surfers, but small kids enjoy jumping them. Tired of sidewalks, buildings, and traffic noise? The landscape here surrounds you with tropical vegetation and the sounds of flowing water. You can also swim through fountains, get splashed by waterfalls, wade in a river, and—most popular among kids—careen through tunnels and down long slides that end with a splash into a pool. (Different

EATS FOR KIDS Aquaboulevard is within the Forest Hills commercial complex, which also contains a branch of family-friendly **Hippopotamus** (tel. 01–53–98–91–20) and fast-food outlets. **Le Bistrot d'André** (232 rue St-Charles, tel. 01–45–57–89–14) is an old-fashioned restaurant serving French home cooking; try the roast leg of lamb. For more on the water theme as well as a splurge, visit the **River Café** (146 quai de Stalingrad, Issy-les-Moulineaux, tel. 01–40–93–50–20), in a nearby suburb. This barge on the Seine is a trendy but friendly restaurant. See also Parc André Citroën.

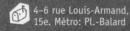 4-6 rue Louis-Armand, 15e. Métro: Pl.-Balard

 €20 ages 12 and up, €10 children 3-11; admission is for 4 hrs

 M-Th 9 AM-11 PM, F 9 AM-12 PM, Sa 8 AM-11 PM, Su 9 AM-11 PM

01-40-60-10-00

 2 and up

age groups have different slides.) Parents aching from too much sightseeing can relax in bubbling hot tubs, and though kids might not need the tubs' therapeutic benefits, they do like the bubbles.

A star attraction here is the life-size model of a whale commissioned by Jacques Cousteau, the late French explorer and film personality who did so much to increase awareness of aquatic environments throughout the world. Because all 27 meters (90 feet) of Madame Whale is hollow, kids can crawl inside and get a close-up look at a whale's inner workings. A gentle slide leading out into a pool is the preferred exit, even for the smallest kids. Children who favor dry land have a special play area where they don't even have to get wet. All in all, the complex is one of the city's best antidotes to stress.

KEEP IN MIND
Aquaboulevard can get extremely crowded. To avoid the crush in July and August, try to come during meal times (noon–2 or 7–9). Note that baggy shorts–type bathing suits for men and boys are not allowed; brief-style swimwear is required.

HEY, KIDS! When you hear a loud toot, it means surf's up—the wave machine is about to turn on. If you happen to be in one of the pools when this happens (after 2:30 only), get ready to ride the waves. When you climb the ladders to the top of the tall water slides, look for the lights, and don't set off until you see the green one. The system was designed so you won't end up sliding down on top of someone else (and so no one will come sliding down on you).

ARC DE TRIOMPHE

One of the world's best-known memorials to military might, this massive monument dates from the early 19th century, but its first years were as up-and-down as the fortunes of the man who had it built.

The Arc de Triomphe (Arch of Triumph) was commissioned by Napoléon in 1806 to commemorate his victory at the Battle of Austerlitz. Little more than the foundations had been finished by 1810, when Napoléon married, so a wood-and-canvas mock arch was erected for the celebrations. When Napoléon lost at Waterloo in 1815, construction was put on hold. The monument was finally finished in 1836, in time for Napoléon's coffin (he had died in 1821) to be hauled through it in a grandiose procession in 1840. Today, the arch is the site of France's Tomb of the Unknown Soldier, where a flame has been kept burning since 1923; it's rekindled every evening at 6:30.

KEEP IN MIND To check out the carvings on the outside of the arch (representing—what else?—war scenes), you'll need to be on the sidewalks on the outer edges of the place Charles-de-Gaulle. The carving entitled *Le départ des volontaires* (Departure of the Volunteers) is considered the best.

EATS FOR KIDS **Alléosse** (13 rue Poncelet, tel. 01–46–22–50–45) is a reliable cheese store on a lively food-market street. **Maison Pou** (16 av. Ternes, tel. 01–43–80–19–24) has served delicious charcuterie since 1830, before the arch was finished. **Lina's Sandwiches** (8 rue Marbeuf, tel. 01–47–23–92–33) has American-style sandwiches, quiches, and salads for here or to go. **Del Papa** (233 bis rue du Faubourg-St-Honoré, tel. 01–47–63–30–98) dishes up tasty pizza, and **La Maison du Chocolat** (225 rue du Faubourg-St-Honoré, tel. 01–42–27–39–44) is chocolate heaven. See also Palais de la Découverte and École Lenôtre.

Pl. Charles-de-Gaulle,
8e. Métro: Charles-de-Gaulle-Étoile

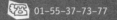 01-55-37-73-77

 €7 adults 26 and up, €4 ages
18–25, 17 and under free;
free entrance first Su of each
month Jan–Mar

 Apr–Sept, daily 9:30 AM–11 PM;
Oct–Mar, daily 10 AM–10:30 PM

8 and up

As far as kids are concerned, though, the most interesting thing about the Arc de Triomphe isn't its history but the view from the top, 45 meters (148 feet) above the place Charles-de-Gaulle (formerly the place de l'Étoile and still called that by Parisians). You can take an elevator, but most children prefer to climb the stairs, all 300 or so of them. Halfway up, a little museum shows a film on the monument's history. From the rooftop terrace you can check out the 12 streets that radiate out from the square, including the avenue Foch, Paris's widest street. You'll see that Paris is bisected by a broad paved line leading straight from the Arc du Carrousel, in front of the Louvre, through the Arc de Triomphe all the way to the Grande Arche in the western suburb of La Défense, with the Champs-Élysées to the east of the arch and the avenue de la Grande Armée to the west. You'll also get a great view of Paris's chaotic traffic swirling nonstop through the square below you.

HEY, KIDS! From the top of the arch, Paris traffic looks totally insane, right? But there is a method to its madness. It's called *priorité à droite*, which means "whoever is on your right has the right-of-way." If you were driving into the place Charles-de-Gaulle, this is how it would work: you'd charge ahead, keeping an eye out for vehicles on your right and doing your best not to hit them. You'd never once look to your left, because whoever was there would be looking at you and staying out of your way. At least that's what you'd be hoping.

Take a trip back in time to the days before Paris was Paris—to the 1st through 3rd centuries AD, when Paris was a bustling Gallo-Roman stronghold called Lutetia, population 6,000. Hidden away behind apartment buildings in the Left Bank district, just off bustling rue Monge, is a city park with a remnant of that time: the Arènes de Lutèce (Lutetia Arena).

Built into a hillside, the arena was used for circus and theatrical productions until around AD 280, when invading barbarians destroyed it and most other Gallo-Roman structures on the Left Bank. For 1,600 years the arena was forgotten, and then at the end of the 19th century its ruins were unearthed during the construction of a line of the Paris métro nearby. The arena's first use after rediscovery, however, was as a parking lot for buses.

Today the Arènes de Lutèce has been excavated and refurbished, but only to the extent that its stonework is now solid and secure. The city wisely chose not to make the ancient

EATS FOR KIDS Pick up some goodies and picnic with Parisians on the arena's stone steps. An open-air market on the place Monge operates Wednesday, Friday, and Sunday mornings, while the nearby rue Mouffetard has an even wider selection of food shops, open Tuesday to Sunday. Especially good bets are **Gelati d'Alberto** (45 rue Mouffetard, tel. 01–43–37–88–07) for luscious ice cream; **La Crêpe Carré** (42 rue Monge, tel. 01–43–26–99–98), for classic main-dish and dessert crêpes; and **Le Jardin des Pâtes** (4 rue Lacépède, tel. 01–43–31–50–71), serving organic vegetarian dishes.

structure into a museum, but rather to give it new life as a public park. The plan worked, and now the arena is one Paris monument that doesn't feel like a monument at all. Locals love to come; tourists rarely seek the place out. Just as thousands of aristocratic Lutetians used to enjoy watching performances here, today's parents enjoy sitting on the stone seats watching their kids play soccer in the arena's sandy ring. Children who don't like soccer love to climb around on the steep stone benches.

The north side of the arena has a cool, shady little park with a gurgling fountain, a play area for smaller kids with a sandbox and jungle gyms, and several benches. That combined with the rest of the arena makes it a perfect spot for a picnic.

KEEP IN MIND

Steep stone stairs and walls without guardrails are dangerous for children under 5, particularly toddlers. Smaller children can safely play on the level court in the center of the arena, however, or in the park and play area on the arena's north side.

HEY, KIDS! Want to know how Paris got its name? A tribe of Gauls called the Parisii lived on what's now the Ile de la Cité (the island in the Seine that's home to Notre-Dame) from the 3rd century BC to the arrival of the Romans in 52 BC. The Romans beat the Gauls and built their own city, Lutetia, which contained the arena, some public baths, a long aqueduct, and other structures. After the barbarians destroyed Lutetia in AD 280, a group of Gauls rebuilt the city and, in 360, named it Paris, in honor of their ancestors.

BATEAUX PARISIENS

Kids can't help but appreciate *bateaux mouches,* the tourist boats that chug up and down the Seine through central Paris. With their big glass roofs and huge spotlights illuminating the city's monuments at night, they look impossibly garish. Once on board, however, you'll be rewarded with a spectacularly beautiful view of the city as seen from the water, a reminder that Paris has been a river port for thousands of years. As for the term *bateaux mouches,* which actually means "fly boats," it comes from the Les Mouches district of Lyon, where the boats were originally manufactured. Of all the tour boat operators—and there are many—a sound choice is Bateaux Parisiens, which is particularly good for the younger set.

Regular cruises begin near the Eiffel Tower and set off for a one-hour voyage that takes you up the river under various bridges, including the Passerelle des Arts (the footbridge leading between the Louvre and the Left Bank), to Notre-Dame on the Ile de la Cité. The boat turns around the island and then heads back downstream past the Louvre

EATS FOR KIDS On a hot summer day, treat yourself to ice cream at **Bac à Glaces** (109 rue du Bac, tel. 01–45–48–87–65). Every possible flavor of ice cream and sherbet is on hand, all scooped into homemade cookie-type cones. See also Tour Eiffel.

KEEP IN MIND Another choice for cruising the Seine is the Batobus (tel. 01–44–11–33–44, www.batobus.com), a leisurely water taxi that makes eight stops. You can get off at any stop, paying according to how far you travel, or take the entire voyage (day pass €10 ages 12 and up, €5.50 children 11 and under; or €3.50 one stop, €2 each additional stop). To find the stops, look for the little Batobus signs along the quais of the Seine. Boats operate April–May and October, daily 10–7, and June–September, daily 10–9.

Port de la Bourdonnais,
7e. Métro: Bir-Hakeim-Grenelle

01–44–11–33–44,
tel. 01–44–11–33–55 meal reservations; www.bateauxparisiens.com

€9 ages 12 and up;
€4.10 children 11 and under; Croisière Enchantée €9.60

 Apr–Oct, daily 10 AM–11 PM every ½ hr;
Nov–Mar, daily 10–10 every ½ hr or hr;
Croisière Enchantée Oct–Mar, Sa–Su 4

All ages; kids' cruises 10 and under

and the Eiffel Tower to tiny Ile des Cygnes (Island of the Swans), which it circles before returning to the dock. Don't miss the replica of sculptor Frédéric-Auguste Bartholdi's Statue of Liberty on the end of the Ile des Cygnes—the real statue was built in Paris in 1886. Throughout the cruise, free headphones let you listen to commentary in a choice of 12 languages, while a loudspeaker blares stirring music in the background. A special commentary for kids 8–14 is available, but only in French. Lunch and dinner cruises with live music give you some of the best dining-room views in Paris, but the meals are not cheap.

On weekends and holidays, a special Croisière Enchantée (Enchanted Cruise) is geared to kids 3–10 and their parents. A pair of elves (professional actors) entertain you by singing songs and telling stories (in French) about the monuments you're sailing past. Now where else can you find singing elves on the Seine?

HEY, KIDS! Paris is divided into Left Bank (Rive Gauche) and Right Bank (Rive Droite), referring to the banks of the Seine from the point of view of a person sailing downstream (with the current). If your boat is traveling upstream toward Notre-Dame and the narration points out the Musée d'Orsay on the Left Bank, you should actually look to your right. The Louvre, on the Right Bank, will be on your left. Got it? Watch people turn their heads back and forth trying to figure out what's going on.

BERCY VILLAGE

Eastern Paris is on the move, with major developments like the Bercy sports and entertainment complex, a Frank Gehry–designed building set to become the new Paris cinema museum, the national library, and now Bercy Village, where a once-scruffy collection of *chais* (wine depots) on the city's eastern edge has been turned into a popular destination for families. You'll find plenty of diversions and room for kids to run around.

Many of the wine-storage facilities, in use since the early 19th century and classified as historic landmarks, now house branches of some of Paris's trendiest shops, most of which offer activities for kids on Wednesdays and Saturdays. All cluster around an attractive courtyard, the Cour Saint Emilion. Bercy Village also regularly organizes very lively treasure hunts for kids 4–10, with clues in French.

The Bercy Village complex is at the eastern end of the 25-acre Parc de Bercy, Paris's newest major park, which contains century-old trees, a pond with curved bridges over it, several

KEEP IN MIND Contact Club Med World (tel. 01–44–68–70–00) for kids' sports classes, Nature et Découvertes (tel. 01–53–33–82–40) for family-oriented nature activities, FNAC Junior (tel. 01–44–73–01–58) for activities related to books and music, Musées et Compagnie (tel. 01–40–02–98–72) for arts-related activities, and Animalis (tel. 01–53–33–87–35) for classes related to animal life. All are on the Cour Saint Emilion. The Musée des Arts Forains is open to groups only, but you can request to be part of a group (tel. 01–43–40–16–15). La Guinguette Pirate (tel. 01–56–29–10–20) is moored at 11 quai François-Mauriac, 13e.

Cour Saint Emilion, 12e. Métro:
Cour-Saint-Emilion

 Free

Daily 24 hrs

01–40–02–90–80;
www.bercyvillage.com

All ages

kids' play areas, and lots of sidewalks where Parisian kids love to roller-skate. In a gesture to the area's wine-oriented past, there's even a vineyard. The Maison du Jardinage (House of Gardening), near the center of the park, schedules classes in gardening for kids and adults year-round (in French; tel. 01–53–46–19–30).

One of the wine depots is home to Le Musée des Arts Forains (Museum of Circus Arts) and its fascinating collection of circus-related items. Another top attraction, anchored just across the Seine from the Parc de Bercy, is La Guinguette Pirate, an authentic Chinese junk that's been turned into a restaurant, theater, and nightclub. Special shows for kids are given (in French, €6.50) on Wednesdays and Saturdays. Most kids will think that seeing La Guinguette Pirate is worth the long walk from Bercy Village even if you don't go to one of the shows, especially since you can board the boat to have a snack. As the French say, *Ça bouge à Bercy* (Bercy is where it's happening).

HEY, KIDS! A Chinese junk is *not* a piece of junk. It's an ancient type of Chinese sailboat whose name comes from an Indonesian word, *jong*. Paris's La Guinguette Pirate junk, built in China in the 1980s, sailed around the world several times before dropping anchor along the Seine in 1995.

EATS FOR KIDS All the Bercy Village restaurants on the Cour Saint Emilion welcome families. Possibilities include **Compagnie de Crêpes** (tel. 01–43–40–24–40) for main-dish and dessert crêpes; **Partie de Campagne** (tel. 01–43–40–44–00) for tasty meals all day; **The Frog at Bercy** (tel. 01–43–40–70–71), a microbrewery and pub; **Hippopotamus** (tel. 01–44–73–88–11), which specializes in grilled meats and fries; **Club Med World** (tel. 01–44–68–70–00) for international dishes with kid appeal; and **T pour 2** (tel. 01–40–19–02–09), a tearoom. **La Guinguette Pirate** also serves meals and snacks.

BOIS DE BOULOGNE

The vast Bois de Boulogne (Boulogne Woods) was once a wild, dangerous forest where the kings of France hunted wolf, deer, and wild boar. (It's still unwise to venture into its wooded areas at night.) Napoléon III gave the forest to Paris in the mid-19th century, and developer Baron Haussmann, who was carving huge boulevards through the city at the time, laid boulevards through the woods as well, modeling his plan on London's Hyde Park. Today, the park is popular among Parisians looking for fresh air and open spaces.

At the Lac Inférieur (the larger of the park's two lakes), you can rent paddleboats, and at the Lac Supérieur, kids bring remote-controlled boats and buzz them around the lake. The park also contains two race courses: the Hippodrome d'Auteuil (tel. 01–70–71–47–47), which stages steeplechases (with jumps and hurdles) regularly March–December, and the Hippodrome de Longchamp (tel. 01–44–40–75–00), which hosts flat racing April–October. On the first Sunday in October, you can watch top Thoroughbreds compete in the world's richest horse race, the Arc de Triomphe.

KEEP IN MIND Although many of the Bois de Boulogne's attractions are near métro stops, you'll need a car or bicycle to tour the whole park. Bikes can be rented near the entrance to the Jardin d'Acclimatation (see #44) and near the boat ramp at the Lac Inférieur.

EATS FOR KIDS Within the park are three worthwhile restaurants. The **Relais du Bois de Boulogne** (carrefour Croix-Catalan, tel. 01–42–15–00–11), in a gorgeous setting, has a popular fixed-price buffet, a children's play area, and a petting zoo. **L'Auberge du Bonheur** (allée de Longchamp, tel. 01–42–24–10–17) has a beautiful outdoor terrace, an indoor fireplace, and reasonable prices. Reservations aren't taken, so arrive by 12:30 for lunch and 7:30 for dinner. Take a little boat to **Le Châlet des Iles** (tel. 01–42–88–04–69), a magical—and expensive—restaurant on the island in the Lac Inférieur.

Main entrances: Porte Maillot, Porte de la Muette, Porte de Passy, 16e. Métro: Porte d'Auteuil, Porte Dauphine, Porte de la Muette, Porte de Passy

 08-36-68-31-12 Office de Tourisme; www.parisbienvenue.com

 Daily 24 hrs

Free

All ages

There is a bird sanctuary near the Grande Cascade (an artificial waterfall), and the gorgeous Parc de Bagatelle contains a little château built in 1755 by the Count d'Artois, Marie Antoinette's brother-in-law; it now displays temporary art exhibits. But this area's main draw is its fabulous flowers, especially the irises in May and the roses in June. While parents relax and take in the blooms, kids can run off steam or have a close encounter with the resident birds—shy ducks and proud peacocks, who roam around spreading their tails and screeching.

The Pré Catalan garden, in the park's center, has kids' play areas and includes the Jardin de Shakespeare, with plants mentioned in the Bard's plays. In summer, open-air Shakespeare productions (some in English) are held near here. The bois's grassy open areas attract Paris-based U.S. expats, who come to play baseball and football, and French people who play soccer and rugby. And there's plenty of room for just running around.

HEY, KIDS! Steeplechase racing has been held at the Hippodrome d'Auteuil since 1870. Why do they call it steeplechasing? Centuries ago in England, horses and riders would race from one village's church steeple to another, jumping over hedgerows and fences along the way. Today's obstacles are built to look like the ones from those old courses: fence-like hurdles, tall jumps covered with tree branches, and even wide ditches. If you go to a race at Auteuil, follow the crowds (with your parents!) to the middle of the course to get a close-up view of the huge horses pounding past you.

BOIS DE VINCENNES

62

Just east of Paris's city limits, the 500-acre-plus Bois de Vincennes (Vincennes Park) is the city's biggest park and well worth a métro ride. Contained within its borders are a number of terrific attractions for kids and families, both indoors and out.

In the former category, the imposing Château de Vincennes, built in the 1300s in the middle of what was once a royal hunting preserve, is worth a visit for its sumptuous gilded interiors. You'll find more gilt on a huge statue of Buddha—the largest in Europe—in a Buddhist temple overlooking the Lac Daumesnil.

Most of the Bois de Vincennes's best attractions, however, are outdoors. Besides the Parc Zoologique de Paris and the Parc Floral de Paris (see #10 and #12), you can explore three lakes: the Lac de Saint Mandé, the Lac Minimes, and the Lac Daumesnil, around which you can watch a puppet show, take a turn on a merry-go-round, eat *barbe à papa* (cotton

HEY, KIDS! Try imagining some of what's happened in the Bois de Vincennes in its long history. The word Vincennes comes from Vilcena, the name of a huge primeval forest (with wild animals and bandits) that existed here in Gallo-Roman times. In the 9th century, monks began holding a fair in the area, and a fair still takes place every year (Easter through May), though it's now called the Foire du Trône and the fair is mainly a huge amusement park with roller coasters. In the 13th century, France's great king St. Louis judged criminals under an enormous, ancient oak tree in the Vincennes woods.

Main entrance: av. Daumesnil, 12e. Métro: Porte Dorée, Château de Vincennes, Porte de Charenton

 08-36-68-31-12 Office de Tourisme, www.parisbi-envenue.com; 01-43-28-47-63 Ferme de Paris

 Park free, some attractions charge

 Daily 24 hrs; attraction hrs vary

 All ages

candy), rent a paddleboat, or just sit on a bench and watch the world go by. Bike lanes, jogging paths, and sidewalks popular with rollerbladers and skateboarders crisscross the park. You'll find plenty of places to picnic as well as huge expanses of grass for running, walking, and even rolling; a number of soccer fields; bike-rental outfits (near the Château de Vincennes and the Lac Daumesnil); and other sports facilities such as the Hippodrome de Vincennes (a horse-racing track).

A young couple runs the kid-oriented Ferme de Paris (rte. de Pésage, near the Hippodrome), a real working farm. Children can sometimes help feed the animals—pigs, chickens, goats, lambs, and more—and there are an orchard, a vegetable garden, and fields of wheat and sunflowers, which are harvested by tractor.

KEEP IN MIND Though patrolled, the park can attract unsavory types. Avoid coming here at night, and be careful where you picnic; sometimes the lawns are not clean. It's best to keep to areas within sight of other people, especially groups.

EATS FOR KIDS The many snack bars and small cafés clustered around the Lac Daumesnil and the Lac des Minimes include **Le Chalet des Iles** (on an island in the Lac des Minimes, tel. 01-43-07-77-07), which has an outdoor terrace. The Bois de Vincennes also makes a great picnic destination; in city "parks" access to grass is usually strictly controlled, but in these "woods" you can spread out as much as you like and actually sit on the lawn. Pick up treats at a charcuterie (take-out meat and food shop) or pâtisserie (pastry shop), and choose a spot.

CATACOMBES

6

You don't have to have ghoulish tendencies to appreciate a visit to Paris's underground graveyard, but it helps. Walk down 90 steps to a huge complex of subterranean caverns stacked floor to ceiling with skeletons—around 6 million of them. Most have been artfully arranged, with row upon row of skulls set upon crossed tibias. The overall effect is like being on the set of a horror movie, reinforced by the title "The Empire of the Dead" indicated on the catacomb's brochures. Guides try to play down the macabre aspects, but with all those skeletons, what can they do?

Originally quarries, the catacombs yielded rocks used in the great buildings, roads, and aqueducts of the pre-Paris, Gallo-Roman stronghold of Lutetia. The quarries had been largely forgotten when, in 1785, someone had the idea to solve the problem of Paris's overcrowded cemeteries by placing skeletons in the underground caves. Several million skeletons from the La Cimetière des Innocents (Cemetery of the Innocents) and others were then hauled here.

KEEP IN MIND You should judge whether your kids are likely to be intrigued or scared by all the bones. Guides light your way as you tour the shadowy caverns, but it's a good idea to bring your own pocket flashlight, as well as a jacket.

HEY, KIDS! The French resistance fighters who made the catacombs their Paris headquarters during World War II were a highly organized group of spies within their own country. In 1940, Germany occupied Paris, controlling the city until France's allies, American and British troops, liberated it in 1944. During the German occupation, some Parisians chose to collaborate with the Germans, while others fled or organized undercover resistance to German rule. Working in small groups whose members usually did not know each others' real names, the Résistance fighters spied on the Germans, sheltered escaped prisoners, and staged sneak attacks.

1 pl. Denfert-Rochereau,
14e. Métro: Denfert-Rochereau

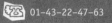 01-43-22-47-63

 €5 adults 27 and up,
€2.50 ages 8–26,
children under 8 free

T 11–4, W–Su 9–4

7 and up

A guide leads you through chilly, cramped corridors—each marked with the name of the street above it—and past stacks of bones. It's as though you're seeing Paris from a ghost's point of view. The indirect lighting casts shadows of bones onto the sides of the tunnels, reinforcing this Halloween atmosphere. Perhaps the most impressive aspect of the catacombs is their size, especially when you realize that you are taken through only a small part of a vast subterranean world with 65 kilometers (40 miles) of tunnels.

A small catacombs museum comes as a relief after your walk through the world of bones. Displays on the long history of this strange Paris underworld include its use as a secret headquarters of the Résistance (French resistance fighters) during Paris's occupation by German troops during World War II. Around 50,000 visitors tour the catacombs every year and survive, proving that there are no dangers here, just the thrill of glimpsing Paris's creepy side—a far cry from the lively boulevards just a few feet above.

EATS FOR KIDS **La Pâte à Crêpes** (19 rue Daguerre, tel. 01–43–20–20–79) specializes in yummy main-dish *galettes* (tarts) and dessert crêpes, always a hit with kids. **Le Zeyer** (234 av. du Maine, on pl. d'Alésia, tel. 01–45–40–43–88), a big, bustling brasserie, prepares delicious sole *meunière* (sole in butter sauce), classic steak-frites (steak with french fries), and *tarte Tatin* (upside-down apple tart). For a taste of home, visit **McDonald's** (5 av. Général-Leclerc, tel. 01–43–22–35–53). See also Médaillons d'Arago.

CATHÉDRALE DE NOTRE-DAME-DE-PARIS

Small children may be disappointed not to see the Disney version of Quasimodo, the Hunchback of Notre-Dame, scrambling around on the cathedral's rooftops, but at least they can check out the gargoyles. France's most famous cathedral was built from 1163 to around 1345 on a spot that had already been considered holy for centuries. Take time to walk all the way around the cathedral to view the spectacular rose window above the main entrance; the gargoyles; the flying buttresses, added in the 14th century to support the structure's walls so that larger windows could be installed; and the magnificent Cloister Portal on the cathedral's north side, created in around 1250. A little park behind the cathedral has swings and benches and is always crowded with mothers, toddlers, and tourists.

Although most of Notre-Dame's original stained-glass windows have been lost over time and the church's interior can get very crowded with tour groups, it's still a thrill to stand within the vast space where for centuries the kings and queens of France were crowned. The main appeal of Notre-Dame for most kids, however, is the chance to climb up to the

HEY, KIDS! Among Notre-Dame's scowling stone gargoyles is one with a trunk. Eons ago, a herd of woolly elephants, *Elephas primigenius*, apparently hung out on the heights of eastern Paris in what is now Buttes-Chaumont park. A tooth from one of these prehistoric creatures was discovered in 1903, when Line 3 of the Paris métro system was being installed. Archaeologists have determined that the trail the elephants followed down to the Seine to drink ended up just across the river from where Notre-Dame stands today, so it's appropriate that there's one stone elephant on the cathedral. Can you find him?

cathedral's roof. The stairs—which are steep and plentiful—begin at the base of the north tower. The reward for your climb (255 steps to the first level, then 125 to the top of the south tower) is a spectacular view of the Seine and the Ile de la Cité. Above you, in the south tower, the cathedral's great bell, known as Emmanuel, weighs 13 tons and is tolled only on momentous occasions.

In front of the church, the square known as the Parvis (from "Paradise") is the place to which all signposts throughout the country refer when they give distances to Paris. Beneath the Parvis, the aptly named *crypte archéologique* has vestiges of Gallo-Roman rooms. To get the best view of the front of Notre-Dame, cross the Pont au Double in front of the cathedral and head to the Left Bank's peaceful little square Viviani. Here you can gaze at this great architectural treasure while having an impromptu park-bench picnic.

KEEP IN MIND

Paris's poignant monument to Parisians deported by the Nazis during World War II stands in the square de l'Ile de France, at the very tip of the Ile de la Cité, behind Notre-Dame. The memorial contains the tomb of the unknown deportee.

EATS FOR KIDS

Le Kiosque Flottant (quai Montebello, tel. 01–43–54–19–51), a restaurant in a houseboat, has choices from breakfast to midnight snacks. **Hippopotamus** (9 rue Lagrange, tel. 01–43–54–13–99), a restaurant chain geared to carnivores, offers crayons, balloons, and a good fixed-price kids' menu. The **Crêperie des Arts** (27 rue St-André-des-Arts, tel. 01–43–26–15–68) creates crêpes of all kinds, from main-dish *galettes* to dessert crêpes. At **La Fourmi Ailée** (8 rue du Fouarre, tel. 01–43–29–40–99), a tearoom/restaurant/library, you can select among salads, vegetarian lasagna, and fine pastries.

CENTRE DE LA MER

Let's hit the beach—or rather the ocean—right here in the heart of Paris! This oceanographic center founded in 1906 by Prince Albert I of Monaco is aimed at making people—especially kids—more sensitive to life forms in marine and other aquatic environments. The center has six aquariums (from 500 to 4,000 liters) that show different types of sea creatures in their natural habitats, from the cold waters of the Atlantic to a tropical coral reef. All are filled with vividly colored animal and plant life sure to please children.

Some of the museum's exhibits are accessible even to very small kids. In the "Qui mange qui?" ("Who eats whom?") display, kids line up picture blocks to see which organisms are at the top and bottom of the food chain. In the "A qui sont ces beaux yeux?" ("Whose pretty eyes are these?") exhibit, youngsters try to match up photos of creatures' eyes with photos of the whole creatures. When you get it right, a bell rings.

KEEP IN MIND Although most of the center's documentation is in French, the fish and turtles themselves require no translation. In addition, many exhibits are very tactile, so even non-French-speaking kids should thoroughly enjoy their visit.

EATS FOR KIDS **Polidor** (41 rue Monsieur-le-Prince, tel. 01–43–26–95–34) is a Paris institution, known to generations of tourists and locals as a good bet for inexpensive family-style French cooking served at big, family-size tables. You may get routed into the back room, where foreigners are often seated, but never mind; just dig in. **Le Jardin des Pâtes** (4 rue Lacépede, tel. 01–43–31–50–71) has organic, vegetarian dishes that include full-flavored soups, pasta with vegetables, and eggy, fruit-filled *clafouti* (a puffy pancake) for dessert. See also Jardin des Plantes, Jardin du Luxembourg, and Muséum National d'Histoire Naturelle.

195 rue St-Jacques,
5e. RER: Luxembourg

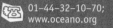 01–44–32–10–70;
www.oceano.org

€4.60 adults, €3 youths
12–18, €2 children 3–11

 T–F 10–12:30 and 1:30–5:30, Sa–Su
10–5:30; closed 3 wks in Aug

 4 and up

A big amphitheater presents films (in French) of the Jacques Cousteau team conducting experiments all over the world and educational puppet shows during France's two-week-long February, Easter, and November school vacations. The center also puts on special temporary exhibits throughout the year.

One of the most thought-provoking exhibits here is the turtle orphanage: a terrarium filled with turtles of various sizes. The center makes a policy of taking in turtles that were bought as pets and then abandoned when they became too big or too aggressive. In so doing, it hopes to educate children about the responsibilities of asking for and caring for a pet, just as it hopes to educate all visitors about their impact on marine life.

HEY, KIDS! As far as clown fish go, it takes all kinds. They all prefer to live in very close quarters with hospitable sea anemones, though. Among *Amphiprion percula* clown fish, one fish in the school (call him a bully) always grows a lot bigger than the others. He hogs the biggest anemone, while his schoolmates may go homeless. *Amphiprion perideraion*, on the other hand, is a family-oriented clown fish, with mom, dad, and the kids sharing an anemone. *Chormis viridis* is a single parent—a dad who gets an anemone ready and raises his kids there alone.

CENTRE NATIONAL D'ART ET DE CULTURE GEORGES POMPIDOU

The Centre Pompidou (Pompidou Center in English, but referred to by Parisians as "Beaubourg," after its neighborhood) was a big city-planning gamble. Former president Georges Pompidou and crew picked a vacant lot in the middle of Paris as the site for a "supermarket for culture" and proceeded to create an edifice that looks like a kid might have built it using Legos and Tinkertoys. Today the recently renovated center is popular among all sorts of Parisians, including children, who come for all sorts of reasons.

Thanks to its wacky architecture, the center is a hit with kids as soon as they see it. From the exterior, you see brightly painted ducts and supports, clearly showing why Parisians nicknamed this place "Notre-Dame des Tuyeaux" ("Our Lady of the Pipes"). Kids also appreciate the big square in front, which is always filled with fire-eaters, sword-swallowers, mimes, and musicians. It's an ongoing, free outdoor circus.

Visitors flock inside to do research in the public library, see films in the movie theaters or

EATS FOR KIDS The center's top-floor **Restaurant Georges,** reached by the glass-walled elevator, has great views and tasty dishes, while the in-house **Café** and **Café-teria** offer lots of low-priced choices. Spacious, popular **Café Beaubourg** (120 rue St-Martin, tel. 01–48–87–63–96) is another choice for sandwiches, light meals, pastries, and drinks. **Dame Tartine** (2 rue Brisemiche, tel. 01–42–77–32–22) serves quiches, salads, and other affordable treats. You can sit outside next to the wacky fountain in square Igor Stravinsky and let the kids run around. See also Jardin des Halles, Musée de la Poupée, Musée Picasso, and Place des Vosges and the Marais.

Rue Beaubourg, 4e. Métro: Hotel-de-Ville, Rambuteau

 Center free; art museum €5.50 adults 18 and up, €10 for day pass to all exhibits; kids' films €3.

 Center W–M 11–10, art museum W–M 11–9, kids' gallery W–M 11–6

01–44–78–12–33, 01–44–78–44–22 Cinema 2; www.centrepompidou.fr

3 and up, kids' gallery 6–12

live performances in the new Grande Salle (Large Hall), or view the stunning collection in the Musée National d'Art Moderne (National Museum of Modern Art). Even small children respond to the art here, especially the Alexander Calder mobiles, the weird mechanical structures of Jean Tinguely, Pablo Picasso's *Petite fille sautant à la corde* (*Little Girl Jumping Rope*), and the vibrantly colored paintings of Matisse, Léger, and Soutine.

In La Galerie des Enfants, a gallery space geared to kids, you'll find special interactive art exhibits (two per year). A recent show let kids discover the art of sculpture through hands-on exhibits and activities related to the work of Constantin Brancusi. Every Wednesday at 2:30, the center's Cinema 2 shows films for kids 7 and up (in French, reservations required). And if it's kid-pleasing vistas you're after, take an elevator that runs through a glass tube up the west side of the building. The view is spectacular, especially at sunset.

HEY, KIDS! Check out the crazy fountain in square Igor Stravinsky, next to the center. It was created in honor of the famous musician by two artists with very different styles: Jean Tinguely (robots) and Niki de Saint-Phalle (colorful pieces, including big red lips that will probably squirt you).

KEEP IN MIND For kids, guided tours and arts workshops called "De l'atelier au musée" (based on the current children's gallery exhibit) are held Wednesdays, Saturdays, and school holidays. Kids 6–12 can take one workshop or a three-workshop series (€8 one session, €37 for a series). A recent choice lets kids make their own sculpture in the style of Jean Tinguely. Guided tours for families are offered monthly on a Sunday (€4 per person). These programs are in French. For information and reservations, visit the ground-floor Espace Éducatif desk or call 01–44–78–49–13.

CHAMPS-ÉLYSÉES

57

If there's one Paris street that people have heard of, it's the avenue des Champs-Élysées—Les Champs to Parisians. This wide street, whose name (translation: "Elysian Fields") suggests paradise, is a paradise for shoppers, window-shoppers, and strollers eager to be part of the action.

Once known as the most beautiful avenue in the world and a popular setting for 19th-century Parisian family outings, the boulevard evolved into a bustling, high-rent commercial district whose sidewalks became parking lots. (As proof, note that the Champs-Élysées is the French Monopoly equivalent of Park Place.) In the past decade, efforts have been made to restore some of the avenue's former beauty by planting trees and reclaiming the sidewalks for pedestrians. Families have returned, and the sidewalks are once again wide enough to walk, push a stroller, and even toddle without getting jostled by other pedestrians—not the case on most Paris streets. Shopping options

HEY, KIDS! Not surprisingly, Paris's oldest Guignol puppet theater has its oldest Guignol puppet, and he's worth more than a lot of the avenue's fancy jewelry. (Guignol is the character with the long black ponytail.) You can recognize him by his green and red jacket; other Guignols wear brown jackets.

KEEP IN MIND Keep a close eye on children as you walk the avenue. Car traffic on the cross streets can be heavy and fast, as can skaters, cyclists, and skateboarders. Keep an eye on the clock and calendar, too. Guignol puppet shows (€2.50) are performed Wednesday, Saturday, Sunday, and holidays at 3, 4, and 5. The stamp and pin market goes into action on Thursday, Saturday, Sunday, and holidays. Note that the big movie theaters on the Champs-Élysées often show films in English with French subtitles. If a U.S. film is billed as "v.o." (*version originale*), it's being shown in English.

Pl. de la Concorde to Arc de Triomphe,
8e. Métro: Franklin-D.-Roosevelt, George-V,
Champs-Élysées-Clemenceau

 Free

Daily 24 hrs

 08–36–68–31–12 Office de Tourisme;
www.parisbienvenue.com

All ages

appeal to all ages, from an enormous Virgin Megastore (#52) for preteens and teens to a Disney Store (#44) for character-loving youngsters. On foot, you'll realize something you probably wouldn't notice from a car: the Champs-Élysées has a fairly steep slope from the place de la Concorde up to the Arc de Triomphe. Keep this in mind if you've got toddlers or a stroller along, and start your journey from the Arc.

At the place de la Concorde end, you'll find the Jardins des Champs-Élysées. Here you can take the kids to Les Marionnnettes du Rond-Point des Champs-Élysées, Paris's oldest Guignol puppet theater (founded 1818), or check out the lively stamp and pin market. But beware: though stamp collectors might love examining the wares, prices are high. You can also take a peek through heavily guarded gates at the Palais d'Élysée (France's White House) and at the nearby U.S. Embassy, on the avenue Gabriel.

EATS FOR KIDS Chic **Fouquet's** (99 av. des Champs-Élysées, tel. 01–47–23–50–00), one of Paris's best-known restaurants, has a classy (and pricey) Sunday jazz brunch that includes a copious kids' menu as well as lively jazz. **Aux Pains Perdus** (39 rue de Berri, tel. 01–43–59–10–96) is a reliable sandwich shop, though its high stools aren't convenient for small kids. See also the Arc de Triomphe, Jardin des Tuileries, and Palais de la Découverte.

CHÂTEAU DE VERSAILLES

To kids, the Château de Versailles and its over-the-top gilded luxury may seem more like a theme park than the palace of French kings. While most children aren't overly impressed by its rich furnishings and sumptuously decorated rooms, they do find much to interest them, both in the château and especially outside it.

Even kids can't resist the dazzling Galerie des Glaces (Hall of Mirrors); the Salon d'Apollo (Throne Room), dripping with gold; and the Chambre du Roi (King's Bedroom), big enough for an army. Watch for images of the sun, in honor of Louis XIV (the Sun King). Louis was jealous of another chateau, Vaux-le-Vicomte, which belonged to his own finance minister. So he had Versailles built, using the same architect (Le Vau), to prove who was boss.

Outside the château, a vast formal garden—created by the architect Le Nôtre (designer of Vaux-le-Vicomte's gardens and Paris's Tuileries)—is filled with statues, fountains, and elegant perspectives. The garden and surrounding park make great places to run off steam. You

KEEP IN MIND Individual audio guides, available in English and for rent at the château's main entrance, help you keep the château's history and contents straight. Kids like wearing the earphones. Guided tours of both the château and park are available in English, but if you understand French, consider the excellent tours for kids and families as well as special kids' workshops (tel. 01–30–83–77–47). Don't miss Les Grandes Eaux Musicales, when the park's fountains are turned on and set to music (May–September, Sunday at 11, 3, and 5:20), and the Grande Fête de la Nuit sound–and–light extravaganzas held in summer.

Town of Versailles

 Château €7.50 ages 18 and up, ages 17 and under and after 3:30 free; Petit Trianon and Hameau de la Reine €5 ages 18 and up, ages 17 and under free; park free

 Château June–Sept, T–Su 9–6; Oct–May, T–Su 10–5; park daily sunrise–sunset

01-30-84-74-00, 01-40-67-10-04 mock farm; www.chateauversailles.fr

3 and up

can tour the park by bicycle (rentals at the porte St-Antoine entrance and near the Grand Canal) or on a little mock train that starts from the château's north terrace, a great option for tired little—or big—feet. Paddling a four-person boat around the Grand Canal is also fun (March–October, rental stand at La Petite Venise). The château's restored Grandes Écuries (Great Stables) have become a school of equestrian arts that presents shows to the public.

Louis XV built the Petit Trianon, an elegant little château in the park, for his mistress, Madame de Pompadour; the ill-fated King Louis XVI later gave it to Marie-Antoinette. Young kids like the Hameau de la Reine (Queen's Hamlet), a mock farm created by Marie-Antoinette so she could play at being a farm woman (albeit one surrounded by servants). Today, at the petting zoo here, kids 5–12 who'd like to play at being Marie-Antoinette can sign up for an afternoon (Wednesday–Saturday) of brushing a donkey and feeding chickens.

GETTING HERE
Versailles is 20 kilometers (12 miles) southwest of Paris. Take the RER commuter train, line C, to the Versailles–Rive Gauche stop; around 60 trains a day run Monday–Saturday, and 35 on Sunday. By car (30 minutes), take the A13 highway west to the Versailles-Château exit.

EATS FOR KIDS **La Flotille** (tel. 01–39–51–41–58), next to the Grand Canal, has a restaurant section (lunch only) with a good fixed-price menu for parents and a tasty kids' menu, as well as a cheaper brasserie section (open all day) with lots of choices. In summer you can eat on the outdoor terrace overlooking the canal. The park also has several snack stands. At **Sister's Café** (15 rue des Réservoirs, tel. 01–30–21–21–22), a relaxed, friendly restaurant, you can sample U.S. treats like chicken wings, quesadillas, and a hearty brunch in the domain of the Sun King.

CITÉ DE LA MUSIQUE

Ever had a yen to play in a gamelan (an Indonesian orchestra)? At the Cité de la Musique (Music Center) complex, the whole family can take a gamelan class as well as attend a concert featuring some of the world's best musicians, check out Beethoven's very own clavichord, and see about 4,500 rare musical instruments from around the globe. Also home to France's prestigious Conservatoire Nationale de Musique (National Music Conservatory), the Cité de la Musique is another jewel in the crown of Paris's ambitious La Villette development project. It's a must for music-lovers.

The center's Musée de la Musique (Music Museum) contains the conservatory's huge collection of musical instruments as well as scale models of opera houses and concert halls with all their backstage equipment. Everything in this museum is designed with kids in mind. As you enter the museum, you receive headphones equipped with an infrared device that senses when you're standing in front of an instrument and starts a tape with commentary and an extract of a virtuoso player's performance on the particular

HEY, KIDS!
What's the difference between a harpsichord and a piano? They both have strings, but the strings of a harpsichord are plucked when keys are played, while in a piano, the strings are hit with little hammers. See if you can hear the difference through your headphones.

EATS FOR KIDS **Café de la Musique** (213 av. Jean-Jaurès, tel. 01–48–03–15–91), a big, relaxed, friendly, and trendy brasserie, serves classic French cuisine (lots of grilled meat), homemade fries, inventive salads, and a good Sunday brunch. The huge terrace is popular on sunny days. **Le Bistrot du Cochon d'Or** (192 av. Jean-Jaurès, tel. 01–42–45–46–46), the more reasonably priced bistro branch of a famous local restaurant, is a carnivore's delight, harking back to the days when La Villette was Paris's slaughterhouse district. See also Cité des Sciences et de l'Industrie and Parc de la Villette.

221 av. Jean-Jaurès,
19e. Métro: Porte-de-Pantin

01–44–84–46–00, 01–44–84–44–84
concerts and classes;
www.cite-musique.fr

Museum €6.10 adults,
€4.60 children 6–18;
concerts and classes vary

T–Su 10–6, to 8 for concerts

7 and up

instrument. Headphones with commentary in English are available. Often kids don't want to take off the headphones when their visit ends. Special guided visits (in French) bring the world of music to life through games and stories, and classes for kids or kids and their families are offered regularly. Children ages 6 and up, for example, can learn how to play the steel drums and really impress their friends back home. Spectacles Jeune Publique (theater-music-dance performances for young audiences) are organized almost every week. After the show, kids usually get to sit and chat with the performers.

As for those gamelan classes, they're for anyone 7 or over who'd like to learn to play one of the 20 or so gamelan instruments. Never played an instrument before? Don't worry; sit on the floor and let the friendly teachers (most of whom speak English) explain the gongs, xylophones, drums, and other Indonesian instruments. After a while, you'll hear yourself and your family making music together. Music is the universal language, after all, and the center is a great place to learn how to speak it.

KEEP IN MIND Atelier de Gamelan en Famille (family gamelan workshop) classes are held in French on Sundays, October–June (€6 per adult, €4 per child). You can also take classes in other instruments. Kid-oriented concerts are usually given on Wednesdays at 3 and Saturdays at 11 (€6). On Wednesdays, Saturdays, Sundays, and school holidays, look for classes and special guided tours of the museum. Top musicians perform regularly at concerts in the 1,000-seat concert hall.

CITÉ DES ENFANTS

54

This children's museum within Paris's futuristic Cité des Sciences et de l'Industrie complex (see #53) is without a doubt one of Paris's top stops for kids. Divided into three sections—one for ages 3–5, one for ages 5–12, and one for special exhibitions—the Cité des Enfants takes very seriously the idea that kids should have fun while they learn. Hands-on exhibits are so colorful and exciting that kids tend to run around the whole time, poking and pushing and pulling. Although children must be accompanied by an adult, no more than two adults per family are allowed in at one time, so if you're over 18, you are definitely going to be in the minority here.

Exhibits for younger kids are simple to use as well as instructive, tactile, and fun. A huge hand-operated grain grinder illustrates how wheat becomes flour. A dance floor activates a video camera, so kids can see themselves hop around. At a construction site

KEEP IN MIND The children's museum is open for four or five (depending on the time of year) 90-minute visits each day, usually beginning at 9:30. Only a limited number of people are allowed inside at each session, so it's a good idea to come here first when you arrive at the Cité des Sciences et de l'Industrie and get tickets for the next available session. Better yet, call the day before to make a reservation. Try to avoid Saturday and Wednesday afternoons, when many day-care centers and schools bring groups here and the staff seems to let in more kids than usual.

Cité des Sciences et de l'Industrie, 30 av. Corentin-Cariou, 19e. Métro: Corentin-Cariou

 €5

T and Th–F 9:30–3:30, W and Sa–Su 10–4:30

08-92-69-70-72 for reservations; www.cite-sciences.fr

3 and up

complete with hard hats, little kids can build huge structures with foam bricks, but the real hit is a whole section that lets kids get as wet as they like while diverting flowing water through channels (plastic lab coats provided).

Older kids can check out all sorts of things involving electricity, learn about genes and solar-powered cars, and more. Instructors, some of whom speak English, offer optional 30-minute classes on special subjects, and, through Techno-Cité, 90-minute sessions (Wednesday and Saturday afternoons and school holidays, ages 11–15, €5) in which kids can learn how to build a robot, program a video game, or operate a helicopter flight simulator. How much more fun can learning get?

EATS FOR KIDS

In addition to the food outlets within the museum complex, you'll find shops on the avenue Corentin-Cariou where you can buy picnic goodies to eat in the Parc de la Villette (see #13; also see the Cité de la Musique and Cité des Sciences et de l'Industrie).

HEY, KIDS! Can you curl up your tongue from side to side? If you can't, blame it on your genes, or rather on one particular gene, which controls whether or not you're born with the little muscles at the base of your tongue that allow you to roll it up. Find out more about your genes in the "Découvrir six de tes caractères génétiques" ("Discover six of your genetic traits") exhibit.

CITÉ DES SCIENCES ET DE L'INDUSTRIE

When you first spot the high-tech exterior of this huge museum complex, it's hard to believe that the site was once home to a ramshackle slaughterhouse in one of Paris's grubbiest neighborhoods. The Cité des Sciences et de l'Industrie (Museum of Science and Industry), a product of inspired city planning, shows that Paris has its foot firmly planted in the 21st century. Everything about this place is cutting-edge, from its architecture to its user-friendly exhibits.

The museum's huge, 9,500-square-meter (102,000-square-foot) Explora section has almost 20 departments full of interactive gadgets that most of us never got to play with in science class. They're all designed to teach schoolchildren (and adults) about subjects including communication, images, outer space, sounds, math, medicine, oceans, volcanoes, computer science, and the gardens of tomorrow. Top kid hits are the Jeux de Lumière (Light Games), which attract even the most blasé video-game player; a display on sound

HEY, KIDS!
You can see the Mona Lisa's famous smile in her portrait in the Louvre, but here in the Explora's "Images" exhibit, you can actually make the Mona Lisa talk—in your own voice. You can also put yourself into a TV ad or play around with a virtual camera. Don't forget to smile.

EATS FOR KIDS The museum complex contains several places to eat, including a self-service cafeteria within the Cité des Sciences where everyone in your group can taste individual portions of classic French fare. At **La Tartine** (25 av. Corentin-Cariou, tel. 01–40–36–22–81), you'll find a wide choice of sandwiches and some salads. For an authentic 1950s bistro with good food and reasonable prices, try **Le Relais Villette** (25 av. Corentin-Cariou, tel. 01–40–36–91–17). See also Cité des Enfants and Parc de la Villette.

Parc de la Villette, 30 av. Corentin-Cariou, 19e. Métro: Porte de la Villette

 €7.50 adults 26 and up, €5.50 ages 7–25, ages 6 and under free; extra charge for some attractions

 T–Su 10–7

01–40–05–80–00 (English message available); www.cite-sciences.fr

 3 and up

deflectors, which lets you whisper and be heard 15 meters (50 feet) away; and the automobile section, where you can test-drive a car using a simulator. There's even a whole museum, the Cité des Enfants (see #54), just for 3- to 12-year-olds.

You could spend days just exploring Explora, but the museum complex offers much more. The gleaming silver Géode dome shows mind-boggling IMAX films on a 1,000-square-meter (over 10,000-square-foot) hemispherical screen, and the 300-seat Le Planétarium presents shows on the galaxy. You can tour the Argonaute, a spy submarine built during the Cold War for the French navy, and check out a space-age greenhouse. The Louis Lumière cinema shows 3-D films (in French and English), and the Cinaxe takes kids on virtual trips, perhaps into outer space or to the bottom of the sea. Cool! This is one museum where your children are almost certain to play happily for hours without whining once—and they're sure to learn something, too.

KEEP IN MIND Long lines can build up at the planetarium and the Géode before each day's shows begin. Both theaters' shows are in French, but the Geode has free headphones with commentary in English. In any case, the images are so stunning that kids should enjoy themselves even if they can't understand the French narration.

DISNEYLAND PARIS & WALT DISNEY STUDIOS PARK

The Magic Kingdom is an easy trip from Paris and a fun break for kids. The resort now includes two theme parks, the original Disneyland Paris and the new Walt Disney Studios Park, which focuses on filmmaking. Between them, you're sure to find something to please everyone in the family.

Disneyland Paris is a reduced version of Disneyland in the United States, but there's still plenty for kids to enjoy. Under-fours will probably be most excited by seeing their favorite Disney characters, who hang out in Town Square every morning and periodically perform at the Théâtre du Château (next to Sleeping Beauty's castle). At 3 PM daily (and again at night), the big Disney parade shows off huge floats based on classic Disney films; grab a spot on the curb of Main Street (and be prepared to defend it against late-arriving, pushy parents and kids). Bigger kids will go for the big-thrill rides: Space Mountain, Indiana Jones and the Temple of Peril: Backwards!, and the Big Thunder Mountain roller

KEEP IN MIND Remember to check rides' height and age restrictions before standing in line. Free Fast Passes allow you to use a special "fast" line for top rides at certain times. Fast Passes are available only in Fast Pass machines next to each ride; to get one, you put your park entrance ticket (your "Passport") into the machine, which will give you a Fast Pass that you can use on that ride. It helps to go to the top rides soon after you enter the park to get your Fast Passes. Note that the Disney hotels within the Disneyland Resort complex are convenient, fun—and expensive.

Marne-la-Vallée

 01-60-30-60-53, 407/934-7639
from U.S.; www.disneylandparis.com

 For each theme park, €36 ages
12 and up, €28 children 3–11;
3-day pass €99 ages 12 and
up, €80 ages 3–11

Apr–June and Sept–Oct, daily 9–8;
July–Aug, daily 9 AM–11 PM; Nov–Mar,
M–F 10–8, Sa–Su 9–8

3 and up

coaster. The Star Tours ride, in Discoveryland, ends in a room filled with computer and video games that any kid suffering PlayStation withdrawal will be glad to see.

In Walt Disney Studios Park, the Catastrophe Canyon ride whizzes you through a film shoot in action, and the Rock 'n' Roller Coaster lets you spin and lurch to the music of Aerosmith. You can also check out some spectacular special effects and see amazing stunts in action. The main drawbacks of either park: younger kids are bombarded with so many stimuli that they may at some point burst into tears through sheer overload, while older kids get frustrated if they have to wait in line for an hour to enjoy a ride that's over in less than four minutes. But everyone forgets these problems when they see the fabulous fireworks display over Sleeping Beauty's castle, with Tinkerbell flitting around overhead leaving a trail of pixie dust.

GETTING HERE

The quickest way (40 minutes) to cover the 32 kilometers (20 miles) from Paris east to Disneyland is by RER commuter train, line A, which stops near the park's gates. Combination Disneyland-transport tickets are on sale in Paris métro and train stations. By car, take the A4 highway toward Marne-la-Vallée; exit at Parc Disneyland.

EATS FOR KIDS Both parks are filled with snack bars and restaurants in a variety of styles and price ranges. **Colonel Hathi's Pizza Outpost** in Disneyland and **Backlot Express** in Walt Disney Studios Park are among the least expensive. Picnicking on food you've brought with you is the cheapest option, but you have to go to the designated picnic areas outside the theme parks' gates to do it.

DOUBLE FOND

You sit down, your waiter brings you a glass of Coke, and—presto!—your glass disappears right before your very eyes! What kind of place IS this?

The Double Fond is a café-theater for people who love magic tricks. (The French name refers to the double, or false, bottom on a trick box.) What sets the shows here apart from big-time magic extravaganzas in huge auditoriums is that the tricks are performed in a fairly small space right in front of you, and everyone in the audience gets a chance to participate. Kids are encouraged to get in on the act, especially at the matinees, designed especially for them. The emphasis is on card tricks and other classic sleight-of-hand numbers that have eternal appeal for youngsters. You and your children can enjoy a part of the city's rich and varied theater scene even if you don't speak French, since the shows are based on gestures rather than language. To get the full benefit of a performance if you don't speak French, ask whether a special show in English can be arranged for a group (call in advance for information). You may be able to join a group that is already scheduled.

EATS FOR KIDS The Double Fond serves drinks but no meals. **Le Studio** (41 rue du Temple, tel. 01–42–74–10–38), for Tex-Mex, has an outdoor courtyard where kids can run around. See also Place des Vosges, Musée de la Curiosité et de la Magie, and Musée Picasso.

KEEP IN MIND Kids' theater in French includes Aktéon Théâtre (11 rue du Générale-Blaise, 11e, tel. 01–43–68–74–62); Antre Magique (50 rue St-Georges, 9e, tel. 01–42–82–13–13); Au Café Chantant (36 rue Bichet, 10e, tel. 01–42–08–83–33), a cabaret; Café-Théâtre les Blancs-Manteaux (15 rue les Blancs-Manteaux, 4e, tel. 01–48–87–15–84); Comédie de Paris (42 rue Fontaine, 9e, tel. 01–42–81–32–22); and Théâtre Fontaine (10 rue Fontaine, 9e, tel. 01–48–74–74–40). Théâtre du Nesle (8 rue Nesle, 6e, tel. 01–46–34–61–04), an English-language theater, sometimes programs plays suitable for kids. See also Opéra Garnier.

1 pl. du Marché-Ste-Catherine,
4e. Métro: St-Paul

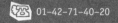 01-42-71-40-20

 €9 matinees,
€16 evenings

June–Sept, daily 8:30 PM, 10:30 PM, and 12 AM
plus Sa 3:30; Oct–May, T–Sa 8:30, 10:30, and
12 plus Sa 3:30

Matinees 6 and up,
evenings 10 and up

You can sit at the tall stools in the downstairs bar with your eyes glued to the magician's hands just inches in front of your face and you still won't be able to tell how the magician manages to make that ace of spades turn up where you least expect it. That is, you probably won't be able to figure it out unless you've taken one of the magic classes offered here (in French). There are special classes for kids (Saturdays 4:30–5:30, €16), as well as classes for adolescents and adults. These classes are only for groups, but you can call ahead to reserve a place with a group. Everyone in the family can learn how to trick your friends back home. Invite a few people over, serve them something to drink, and—you got it!— no more glass. Tell them you learned it in Paris.

For more magic tricks, visit the nearby Musée de la Curiosité et de la Magie (see #34).

HEY, KIDS! Here's a simple card trick. Before you start, arrange a deck of cards with one black four on top and the other black four on the bottom. Fan the cards and ask someone to pick a card and look at it. Then, put the top half of the deck face down on a table and have the person put the selected card on top of it. Put the other half of the deck on top of the card. Then look through the deck. The card in between the two black fours will be the one the person picked.

ÉCOLE LENÔTRE POUR AMATEURS GASTRONOMES

How would you like your kids to whip up a chocolate mousse for your next dinner party? They can learn how to do just that and a whole lot more at this cooking school for kids organized by Lenôtre, one of France's best-known names in gourmet cuisine and pastry.

The 90-minute classes are given on Wednesday afternoons (in French) in a cozy kitchen meant to reproduce conditions in your own home—if your home kitchen runs to marble countertops, blue-and-white-tile walls, and a battery of saucepans in kid-pleasing bright red with white polka dots. Classes, each led by a highly trained Lenôtre chef, are limited to seven kids, so every child gets plenty of chances to ask questions and get to know fellow food-loving classmates. These very hands-on classes show kids how much fun cooking can be, while also teaching them basic techniques of classic French cuisine. Children won't be asked to use any dangerous kitchen equipment (specially designed recipes avoid

EATS FOR KIDS The on-site **Lenôtre** shop sells dozens of take-out goodies. Still hungry? **GR 5** (13 rue Gustave-Courbet, tel. 01–47–27–09–84), named for one of France's main hiking trails, specializes in cooking from mountainous eastern France. Kids should like the stick-to-your-ribs cheese fondue or the raclette (melted cheese cooked at your table on a hot grill); you spread the cheese over boiled potatoes and ham. Don't forget the pickles. **Coffee Parisien** (7 rue Gustave-Courbet, tel. 01–45–53–17–17) does the job when you're homesick for bagels and cream cheese, eggs Benedict, a pastrami sandwich, or cheesecake. See also Arc de Triomphe.

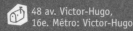 48 av. Victor-Hugo,
16e. Métro: Victor-Hugo

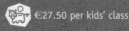 €27.50 per kids' class

 Sept–June, W 2–3:30 or 4–5:30

01–45–02–21–19;
www.lenotre.fr

8–12

the need for that), but will sometimes do some chopping under the chef's watchful eye. The most-used tools are the whisk and the wooden spoon. Note that even though most of the resident chefs speak English, children need to speak at least some French to be able to follow what's going on.

Each class focuses on a particular dish. Some recent classes taught kids how to make *mousse au chocolat* (chocolate mousse), *tartelettes au citron* (lemon tarts), chocolate madeleines (in case someone wants to have a Proustian experience flavored with chocolate), *fondue au chocolat* (chocolate fondue, a very popular offering), and *bûche de Noël* (yule log, a gooey Christmas cake decorated to look like a log). The best part is that kids get to eat their creations after the class and, if there's any left over, bring some home to share with their family.

HEY, KIDS! In a book by the French writer Marcel Proust, a character eats a madeleine cookie and is suddenly overcome with memories of his childhood. Can you think of something to eat that would bring back memories of when you were really little?

KEEP IN MIND For cuisine-loving moms and dads, Lenôtre gives highly rated classes for adults (in French) Monday–Tuesday and Thursday–Saturday. These classes (six or seven people) last 3½ hours or more and cost from around €80 (croissants, for example) to €214 (a gala Christmas dinner). But you do get to eat what you prepare, not to mention wow your and your kids' friends at your next party. For any class, contact the school well in advance to find out what dishes are being taught when and to reserve a place.

LES ÉGOUTS

C ome to Paris and tour the sewers? Yuck! Well, that might be your reaction, but kids seem to be enthusiastic about visiting the city's collective plumbing system. And they're not the only ones; Paris's sewer tour has become so popular that lines for it can get really long in summer. The tour's appeal seems to lie in seeing Paris's flip side: the dark, smelly underbelly of the gleaming, elegant city overhead. Don't worry; you won't have to walk in or touch anything icky.

You visit a small underground museum and an area where you pick up a brochure (English version available) and see a film (in French) on Paris's public sanitation system, from its earliest days to the present. Next, you go on a tour of the sewers in action. Guides take groups through a few well-lit tunnels to show you how the system works (tours in English offered in summer). Each tunnel is marked with the name of the street it serves, and pipes coming from individual buildings are marked with their addresses. As in the Catacombes (see #61), across town, you'll discover that there's a whole world under

HEY, KIDS!
Which city has the world's biggest sewer system? No, it's not New York or Tokyo. It's Chicago! Paris's system is ranked the world's second largest. The visit lets you check out about 4,500 feet of it, a tiny part of the whole network.

EATS FOR KIDS
Thoumieux (79 rue St-Dominique, tel. 01–47–05–49–75), a classic bistro owned by the same family for three generations, prepares homey French dishes at very reasonable prices. With authentic turn-of-the-20th-century decor, **Poujauran** (20 rue Jean-Nicot, tel. 01–47–05–80–88) is one of Paris's best bakeries/pastry shops, famous for its sourdough baguettes, *cannelés* (soft, yeast-risen sweet cakes), and buttery *gâteau basque* (Basque pound cake). Treat yourself to sublime chocolates from **Michel Chaudun** (149 rue de l'Université, tel. 01–47–53–74–40); the peppery *ganache aux poivre* is out of this world. See also Palais de Chaillot and Tour Eiffel.

93 quai d'Orsay, 7e.
Métro: Alma-Marceau

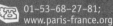 01–53–68–27–81;
www.paris-france.org

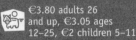 €3.80 adults 26
and up, €3.05 ages
12–25, €2 children 5–11

 May–Sept, M–W and Sa–Su 11–5;
Oct–Apr, M–W and Sa–Su 11–4

6 and up

your feet wherever you go in Paris.

Along the way, you discover that sewers are a fairly recent innovation for Paris. Up until the Middle Ages, the city got its drinking water from the Seine and disposed of its wastes in surrounding fields or by piping garbage and unmentionable refuse through narrow, open channels of packed earth called *ruelles* (a name many small streets still have). Around 1200, King Philippe-Auguste had many Parisian streets paved, with channels running down their middles to carry waste away. During Napoléon's time, underground sewers with arched ceilings were installed, but it wasn't until the 1850s, when Baron Haussmann overhauled the whole city by laying huge boulevards through it, that today's extensive sewer system began to take form. It's mind-boggling to think of how the city must have smelled until that time. You'll get a hint of it from the strong, *je ne sais quoi* smell permeating your tour.

KEEP IN MIND The tour takes an hour (not counting the time spent standing in line to get in), and people with claustrophobic tendencies may be uncomfortable. While you're in the neighborhood, you might want to visit Paris's Église Américaine (American Church; 65 quai d'Orsay, tel. 01–47–05–07–99). In addition to services, the church sponsors or hosts a number of public-service organizations, language classes, and activities for children and families. A bulletin board near the main desk has notices about activities and other subjects of interest to Paris's expat American community.

FONDATION CLAUDE MONET

You can spend a day in the country and enjoy the arts, too, in Giverny, a pretty little village on the bank of the Seine west of Paris that was home to the Impressionist painter Claude Monet from 1883 until his death in 1926. Tops on the list is a visit to Monet's house, now a museum (but called the Claude Monet Foundation), which an international group of Monet fans saved from decay after 1980. You'll get a feel for what life was like when the artist lived and worked here and made the house a gathering place for his artist friends. Coming here also lets kids who've seen Monet's water-lily paintings in the Musée d'Orsay (see #30) make the connection between those works and the real person who created them in the nearby garden.

The first thing you'll notice is Monet's love of color. The house, set in a luxuriant garden, has peachy-pink walls and deep green shutters on the outside. On the inside, rooms have been restored as much as possible to what they were when Monet lived in them. Even small children should like the buttercup-yellow dining room with its big farmhouse table, yellow

KEEP IN MIND Another Giverny attraction, the Musée d'Art Américain (99 rue Claude-Monet, tel. 02–32–51–94–65, http://giverny.org/museums/american), in an elegant contemporary building, holds a permanent collection and changing exhibits of works by American artists with close ties to France. A booklet (in English) takes you on a fun tour. The museum also organizes arts conferences, concerts, and arts-related films (often in English). Through the very popular Ateliers en Plein Air (outdoor painting workshops), anyone over seven can join a small group (maximum 12) and paint in the museum's garden, getting feedback from English-speaking art instructors; reservations are necessary.

59 rue Claude-Monet, Giverny

02-32-51-28-21;
www.fondation-monet.com

 €5.50 ages 19 and up, €4
ages 12–18, €3 ages 7–11,
children 6 and under free

Apr–Oct, T–Su 9:30–6

7 and up

chimneypiece, and Monet's favorite Japanese prints on the walls. Renoir, Sisley, Cézanne, Manet, and Pissarro all came here to share the excellent and copious meals Monet favored, and to debate about art. Kids should appreciate the cheery kitchen, too, with its gorgeous bright-blue Portuguese tiles and more gleaming copper saucepans than you ever thought existed. You can also visit the painter's studio, furnished like a den with armchairs and little tables. Although you'll see no original paintings here now, reproductions of Monet's works hang on the walls to remind you of the images that the artist created in this place.

Kids should enjoy a tour of the garden, with its paths winding through banks of flowers, its water-lily-filled ponds, and its picturesque Japanese bridge immortalized in Monet's works. You'll feel like you've walked inside one of his paintings.

EATS FOR KIDS
Les Nymphéas (48 rue Claude-Monet, tel. 02–32–21–20–31) serves good fixed-price menus, salads, and ice cream. The **Musée d'Art Américain** restaurant/tearoom (see Keep in Mind) offers light meals and afternoon pastries; eat on the terrace and let the kids run in the garden.

GETTING HERE Giverny is 87 kilometers (54 miles) west of Paris. By rail, take the Rouen–Le Havre train from Paris's Gare Saint-Lazare and get off at the Vernon stop, from which you can take a taxi or bus to Giverny, around 5 kilometers (3 miles) away. You can also rent bicycles at the station in Vernon and bike to Giverny. From the train station, cross the bridge over the Seine and turn right. By car, take the A13 autoroute (toll highway) from Paris toward Le Havre, and get off at the Vernon exit. From Vernon, take the D191 and the D5 roads to Giverny.

FRANCE MINIATURE

I f you've ever wished you could visit all of France in a day, now you can. This theme park in a suburb 25 kilometers (16 miles) west of Paris contains more than 150 models of villages, monuments, and other sites from all over France, all carefully re-created at a scale of one-thirtieth the size of the originals. Everything has been done with an attention to detail that can only be described as obsessive.

A reduced version of the real monument's environment surrounds each model, from authentic vegetation right down to the tiniest side street. The real trees and bushes here, 25,000 of them, have been trimmed to one-thirtieth their normal sizes, and the park's landscape designers have made sure that every miniaturized geographical feature represented— every hill, every river—is as accurate as possible. The Château de Versailles surrounded by its gardens looks exactly like the real thing, but smaller, with every turret, fountain, and statue reproduced in a 100-meter (328-foot) display.

EATS FOR KIDS The theme park contains two restaurants, **La Poêlée** and **Les Provinces,** both serving traditional French dishes (normal size) and both with a choice of fixed-price and kids' menus. The park also has a picnic area if you'd like to bring your own goodies.

GETTING HERE France Miniature is in the village of Élancourt, near St-Quentin-en-Yvelines, which is west of Paris near Versailles. By car, take the A13 highway west of Paris, then the A12 toward St-Quentin-en-Yvelines. Follow the signs to France Miniature. By rail from Paris's Gare Montparnasse, take the train to La Verrière; then follow the signs to the France Miniature bus (#411), which takes you to the park. A combined train–bus–park-entrance ticket for France Miniature is available at all Paris train stations.

25 rte. du Mesnil, Élancourt

 €12.50 ages 17 and up, €8.80 children 4–16 , children 3 and under free

 Apr–mid-Sept, daily 10–7; mid-Sept–Nov, M–Sa 10–6, Su 10–7

08–36–68–53–35; www.franceminiature.com

3 and up

It's certainly a little strange to see an Eiffel Tower whose first level you can reach out and touch while you're standing on the ground, but kids will love running around this Lilliputian world, picking out the monuments they recognize. Animated figures, taped sounds, and electronically controlled boats, trains, and cars bring the displays to life. Kids learn something here, too, because the park demonstrates not only France's geography and topography but also the country's great variety of architectural styles from ancient to modern, as well as regional differences. Special events are regularly organized in the park, and brochures (English versions available) help you take your own tours from particular perspectives, such as "Légendes" (legends) or "Gastronomie" (gastronomy).

HEY, KIDS! A team of 53 architects and model-makers created France Miniature's models using real bricks, tile, and stone. These models weren't easy to put together. The model of the Château de Chambord (in the Loire Valley) took 2,000 hours to build, and the model of the Stade de France stadium contains 50,000 lifelike spectators, all painted by hand—and all to scale. The model of the Eiffel Tower, one of the most difficult to build, cost more than €150,000.

HALLE SAINT-PIERRE

Here's an innovative arts center for kids that the whole family can enjoy. Housed in a beautifully renovated 19th-century structure that once was a covered food market, the Halle Saint-Pierre is just off pretty Willette park, which slopes down the steep hillside under Sacré Coeur. Among its many offerings, the center has an exhibition space for temporary shows geared to children and families (one celebrated an imaginary country of colorful nature-worshipers); one-hour *ateliers* (classes) for kids in dance, music, and art; a folk art museum; and other performances and programs of interest to artistically minded kids.

One of the main reasons the Halle Saint-Pierre is popular among Parisian families is the ateliers, which are held all year long on Wednesdays, Saturdays, and during school vacations from 3 to 4 (in French). Classes are usually geared to the special exhibits going on in the center at the time, and children are encouraged to show up an hour early to tour the exhibit before coming to class.

HEY, KIDS! A special Halloween party for kids is held in the Halle Saint-Pierre every year, one sign that Halloween—which is not a traditional French holiday—has taken Paris by storm. The French have their own kind of Halloween, but they celebrate it very differently. It's called Toussaint (All Saints' Day), and it's on November 1. Toussaint is the day when everyone is supposed to remember people who have died, and in the past this meant visiting a cemetery. Until the mid-1990s, most French kids hadn't even heard of trick-or-treating for candy.

2 rue Ronsard, 18e. Métro: Anvers

 Center free; museum €6 adults, €5 children 17 and under, €8 with kids' class

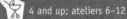 M-Sa 10-6

01-42-58-72-89; www.hallesaintpierre.org

4 and up; ateliers 6-12

Also in the center, the kid-friendly Musée d'Art Naïf Max Fourny contains colorful works of folk art that appeal to even the smallest children. They'll laugh at the big painting of giant crabs pinching people with their huge claws and at the portrait of a troupe of musical monkeys. Guignol puppet shows and theatrical performances for kids (in French) are hosted on Wednesday, Saturday, and Sunday afternoons at 3:30 and 4:30, and special events are organized during Halloween, Christmas, and Easter.

The fun continues just outside the center in the place St-Pierre, a little square where you find a colorful antique merry-go-round and a kids' play area outfitted with a sandbox and climbing equipment. The funicular train that takes you up to Sacré Coeur (see #4) begins in this square.

EATS FOR KIDS
The center's in-house **Café Halle Saint-Pierre** is a popular spot for snacks and drinks. French kids favor *grenadine*, a glass of bubbly water flavored with sweet, red fruit syrup. (You can also order coffee or a Coke.) See also Sacré Coeur and Montmartre.

KEEP IN MIND The children's ateliers are much in demand, so if your kids are interested in participating in one, it's best to call ahead to find out what's being offered and to reserve a place. If you also have children who are too young for the workshops, you can drop the older one off and spend the hour with the younger ones playing in the nearby park or taking them for a ride on the funicular.

HÔTEL NATIONAL DES INVALIDES

45

Topped with the glittering gold dome of the 17th-century Église du Dôme church, Les Invalides (as Parisians call it) originally housed a splendid hospital for invalid soldiers who'd served King Louis XIV. Today, this imposing complex of four elegant pavilions around a huge central courtyard is home to Napoléon's tomb (in the Église du Dôme, commissioned by Louis XIV as a church for visiting aristocracy), the adjoining Église St-Louis-des-Invalides (a smaller, very plain church designed for soldier-patients), and three museums containing largely military exhibits.

Kids should enjoy seeing the imposing blood-red tomb of the brilliant, power-hungry soldier who began his career calling himself a man of the people and eventually appointed himself emperor. Exiled in 1815 after his defeat at Waterloo, Napoléon died in 1821. His body was returned to France for a grandiose funeral in 1840, but his tomb here wasn't ready until 1861. Today, Napoléon lies inside a set of coffins made of mahogany, tin, lead, ebony, and oak. He's not going anywhere.

EATS FOR KIDS The Musée de l'Armée has a **cafeteria. Les Deux Abeilles** (189 rue de la Université, tel. 01–45–55–64–04), a cozy tearoom, prepares omelets, quiches, salads and scrumptious desserts. **The Real McCoy** (194 rue de Grenelle, tel. 01–45–56–98–82) has U.S.-style sandwiches. See also Musée Rodin and Tour Eiffel.

KEEP IN MIND The Musée de l'Armée organizes a number of special activities for kids (in French). In *visites-contes* (visit-stories), children 7–12 and their families are taken around the collection and told entertaining stories about objects (Wednesday and Saturday at 2, €6 adults, €4.50 children). As part of an *armoiries et emblèmes* (coats of arms and shields) workshop, kids create their own personal crests using medieval symbols and colors. *Parcours-découvertes* (discovery map) brochures contain games and questions that help families see the collection in new ways. For information on kids' classes, call 01–44–42–51–73 (reservations advised).

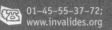

The Musée de l'Armée (Army Museum) displays a vast collection of kid-pleasing weaponry and other military gear: intricate medieval weapons, a suit of armor worn by King Henri II when he was a child, early firearms from the time of Louis XIII, a war outfit once worn by the emperor of China, medieval shields and heraldry, and, for a touch of the macabre, Napoléon's dog, stuffed, in the section of Napoléon memorabilia. The Musée des Plans-Reliefs—literally, a museum devoted to relief maps—is actually a collection of scale models of France's most famous fortified cities, complete with moats and drawbridges. In the Église St-Louis-des-Invalides, you see a set of flags French troops took from their enemies in 19th- and 20th-century battles. The Musée de l'Ordre de la Libération—which is devoted to World War II and especially to France's liberation from Nazi occupation—gives kids who've visited the Catacombes (see #61), secret headquarters of the French Résistance, some background on that movement.

HEY, KIDS! You've probably never seen as many cannons as you'll find in the Musée de l'Armée; they're everywhere. Check out the beautifully decorated 18th-century ones in the central courtyard, one of which is named Le Maniac. If you look inside the barrels of the cannons, you'll see that they're carved in a spiral pattern. This caused the cannonball to spin when it was shot out of the barrel, which made it fly straighter and more accurately. Note the arrows on the cannons; they indicate which end the ball comes out, just in case some soldier got confused.

JARDIN D'ACCLIMATATION

Ready for a ride on a dragon? Want to see a puppet show, scramble up a climbing wall, and try out the latest interactive computer technology, all in one park? Then come to the Jardin d'Acclimatation, Paris's oldest children's amusement park, which has been pleasing kids and their families since 1860.

This park is an engaging mix of old and new. The attractions include a little mini-farm where farm animals roam free; a petting zoo that's home to small, cuddly creatures like miniature goats; a hall of mirrors; and a sedate family of bears. Youngsters especially love these classics, which just goes to show that old-fashioned amusements can still have great kid appeal.

Moving into the 20th century, you have your choice of two roller coasters (the aforementioned dragon, for smaller kids, and a bigger, scarier coaster for bigger, fearless kids), an extremely tame riverboat ride, very untame bumper cars and minicars, a miniature golf course, and

EATS FOR KIDS The park contains snack bars and three restaurants, two of which— **Le Pavillon des Oiseaux** (tel. 01–40–67–92–93) and **La Cheminée du Bowling** (tel. 01– 53–64–93–02)—serve Sunday brunch. In Neuilly-sur-Seine, **Monoprix** (72 av. Charles-de-Gaulle, tel. 01–47–45–24–42) department store sells picnic food; **Lina's Sandwiches** (156 av. Charles-de-Gaulle, tel. 01–47–45–24–42) has U.S.-style sandwiches and salads to eat in or take out, and **Durand Dupont Drugstore** (14 pl. du Marché, tel. 01–41–92–93– 00) serves a copious Sunday brunch and great desserts anytime. See also Bois de Boulogne.

lots of innovative things to slide down or climb up. In the Maison Enchantée, a fairy-tale environment that brings you into the 21st century, older kids can play with high-tech gadgets, toddlers can swim in a pool full of plastic balls, and babies nine months and up can roll around in an *espace mousse* (foam room) just for them. Explor@dome has hands-on science displays and computer games, and the Musée en Herbe (see #28) is a special kids' museum. Activities for kids four and up are organized in the Ateliers du Jardin on Wednesdays and Saturdays.

The park's Théâtre du Jardin hosts kid-friendly concerts, plays and puppet shows, and the Alexandra Bouglione circus is on hand for fans of the Big Top. Is it any wonder that after almost a century and a half, this 9-acre park is still going strong?

HEY, KIDS! Ready to tackle Paris traffic? You'll get a feel for it if you drive one of the park's popular minicars, designed to operate as much as possible like a real automobile, although luckily these cars don't match Paris street speeds. Don't forget to give anything on your right the right-of-way.

KEEP IN MIND The most fun way to arrive at the Jardin d'Acclimatation is to take Le Petit Train from the Porte Maillot (at the edge of the Bois de Boulogne) to the amusement park's entrance. The little steam engine–powered train runs every 15 minutes (11–6) on Wednesday, Saturday, and Sunday and every day during school vacations. A €4.60-per-person round-trip ticket includes park admission. If your kids are interested in the Ateliers du Jardin classes (held in French), reserve in advance (tel. 01–45–00–23–01). Recent classes have focused on cooking, music, colors, and perfume.

JARDIN DE SCULPTURE EN PLEIN AIR

Paris's open-air sculpture garden, in a little public park (Jardin Tino Rossi) next to a cobblestone quai on the Seine, is one art display that won't bore kids. Officially it's called the Musée de la Sculpture en Plein Air de la Ville de Paris, but that's an awfully unwieldy name for one of the city's most accessible art venues. Here monumental sculptures created by some of the most famous artists of the 20th century (Brancusi, Zadkine, César, and others) can be touched, climbed on, and generally treated like familiar objects. In fact, the whole point of this museum is that it doesn't feel like a museum at all. You'll find no barriers between you and the sculptures, and in fact no barriers between you and the Seine, so keep a close eye on toddlers.

The little park is long and narrow, with rambling, curving sidewalks kids like to skate or ride bikes on. Lots of trees, flowers, and park benches fill the park, though as in most

KEEP IN MIND Since this garden is accessible to anyone at any time, unsavory types sometimes hang out here at night. During the day, however, the park is constantly patrolled by guards, who, along with ensuring your safety, ensure the safety of the grass.

EATS FOR KIDS The park's guards don't mind if you picnic on a park bench. You can also cross the river behind Notre-Dame and head for the Ile St-Louis, where you can sample Paris's most famous ice cream at **Berthillon** (31 rue St-Louis-en-Ile, tel. 01–43–54–31–61). You can get a luscious cone to go or sit down in the shop's tearoom, through the door to the right of the take-out window. Try the *gianduja* (chocolate-hazelnut) ice cream. Yum! See also Cathédrale de Notre-Dame-de-Paris, Jardin des Plantes, and Muséum National d'Histoire Naturelle.

Quai St-Bernard, 5e, Métro: Austerlitz

 Free

 Daily 24 hrs

08–36–68–31–12 Office de Tourisme;
www.paris-bienvenue.com

All ages

city parks, you're not supposed to walk or sit on the grass. A big children's play area, with climbing equipment and slides, has a fence around it so little kids can't sneak out while their parents' backs are turned.

The sculpture garden is a favorite spot among Parisians for a Sunday stroll *en famille* before or after a visit to the nearby Jardin des Plantes (see #41). Musicians, joggers, and people pushing sleeping babies in strollers also hang out here, and several houseboats that have been made into living quarters are docked here permanently. On weekends, you'll often see a group of tango fanatics dancing in a paved area next to the river. A special plus is the spectacular view you'll have of Notre-Dame across the Seine, and you won't have to share it with a zillion tour buses.

HEY, KIDS! From the sculpture garden, you can clearly see the so-called flying buttresses on the back of Notre-Dame. These 50-foot-tall stone arches were added to the cathedral in the 14th century to support its walls so that bigger stained-glass windows could be installed. The buttresses don't fly, of course, but in the 14th century, when this church was by far the tallest building in Paris, people must have thought that the soaring buttresses looked as if they might actually take off.

JARDIN DES HALLES

This kid-friendly park in the very center of Paris was created on the spot where the city's central open-air food market, Les Halles, stood for 800 years. That Les Halles, the vibrant and picturesque "belly of Paris," moved to the Paris suburb of Rungis in 1969. Its replacement stretches out in beautifully landscaped sections, with historic Église St-Eustache on its north side. Arched trellises remind Parisian old-timers of the iron arches that rose over the old marketplace, but there the nostalgia stops. This modern park lacks the scruffy charm of the old Les Halles. In its place, it has substituted lots of features that attract children.

Kids like the waterfall, which they can actually get wet in; a fenced-in grassy area just for toddlers and their families; two well-equipped, free play areas with jungle gyms and other climbing equipment; an Olympic-size public pool (in the underground shopping complex beneath the park); and one of Paris's loveliest merry-go-rounds. The drawback:

EATS FOR KIDS **Chicago Meatpackers** (8 rue Coquillière, tel. 01–40–28–02–33) is a top choice when you just have to have a cheeseburger and fries. An electric train circles above your heads, kids get balloons and coloring books, and there's entertainment at lunch. Treat the family to Paris ice cream, pastries, or take-out food at **Stohrer** (51 rue Montorgueil, tel. 01–42–33–38–20), a shop that's been tempting Parisians since 1730; it's on a lively market street. For U.S.-style ice cream, try **Tom and Jerry's** (4 rue Pierre-Lescot, tel. 01–53–40–96–92) or **Häagen-Dazs** (Porte St-Eustache, tel. 01–42–36–15–31).

105 rue Rambuteau,
1er. Métro: Les Halles

 Free; Jardin des
Enfants €3

01-45-08-07-18

 Daily 24 hrs.; Jardin des Enfants T and Th–F
9–12 and 2–6 plus Apr–Oct, W and Sa 10–6,
Su 1–6 (Nov–Mar, Sa 10–4, Sun 1–4)

3–12; Jardin des Enfants
7–12

unsavory characters hang out here, especially at night. The park is very well patrolled, however.

Le Jardin des Enfants des Halles is a small but special park for schoolchildren (7–12) in a corner of the Jardin des Halles. Unlike other Paris children's parks, this one is off-limits to parents, except on Saturday mornings. Friendly trained staff help kids discover six different "worlds" within the little park: the *monde sauvage* (wild world), with canyons, waterfalls, and tiger traps; the *monde volcanique* (volcanic world), where kids can climb up the face of a small artificial volcano, down into its crater, and onto a mysterious island surrounded by water; the *monde mou* (soft world), with a ball crawl to swim in; the *monde géométrique et sonore* (world of geometry and sounds), where scientific experiments deal with numbers and sounds; and the *cité perdue* (lost city), where kids clamber through a labyrinth and into a giant snail.

HEY, KIDS! Parisian kids love to climb on the giant head-and-hand sculpture between the St-Eustache church and the Les Halles fountain, and the open square in front of the head is perfect for throwing a Frisbee. You can wade in a fountain here, too.

KEEP IN MIND The Jardin des Enfants des Halles opens promptly on the hour for only 60 kids at a time (arrive early). Kids can stay only one hour. Parents and children under 7 (with a parent) are only allowed in between 10 and 2 on Saturdays. At other times, young children can call the open play area just in front of the entrance their own, or they can try out one of Paris's oldest and loveliest merry-go-rounds in the southeast corner of the Jardin des Halles near the Jardin des Enfants.

JARDIN DES PLANTES

Paris's centuries-old botanical garden first opened to the public in 1650, and from that time on it's been drawing families in search of a little nature in the city. Thousands of flowers and plants that look beautiful year-round border the wide graveled walkways leading from the Seine to the Muséum National d'Histoire Naturelle complex. Sitting on a bench here and watching the world go by is one of Paris's great free pleasures.

Kids can run off steam along the central garden's wide paths, and a fun children's play area (on the garden's western edge, near the rue Cuvier) contains lots of structures to climb on, including a huge jungle-gym contraption that looks like a dinosaur. On the garden's southwestern edge, winding paths to the summit of a hill form a maze; on the eastern edge of the park near the Museum National d'Histoire Naturelle is the Dodo Manège, a charming merry-go-round that lets little kids ride on models of extinct or endangered animals.

The Jardin des Plantes contains the world's oldest public zoo, La Ménagerie, opened

HEY, KIDS!

The zoo's first elephant arrived in 1795, followed by the first bear, Martin. Ever since, all the zoo's bears have been named Martin in his honor. The zoo's first giraffe, Zarafa, sailed from Africa to Marseilles in 1827 and then walked to Paris.

EATS FOR KIDS You'll see several snacks stands near the zoo entrance as well as the **Restaurant de La Ménagerie,** whose specialty is crêpes, inside the zoo. **Café Maure de la Mosquée de Paris** (39 rue Geoffroy-St-Hilaire, tel. 01–43–31–18–14), adjoining Paris's gleaming white mosque, stands out for mint tea and pastries in the tearoom or couscous (North African stew) in the restaurant. Try the *cornes de gazelle* (gazelle's horn) pastry. **Croq O' Pain** (30 rue Geoffrey St-Hilaire, tel. 01–43–31–24–80) prepares budget-priced and tasty sandwiches and salads. See also Muséum National d'Histoire Naturelle.

57 rue Cuvier, quai St-Bernard,
5e. Métro: Pl. Monge

 01–40–79–30–00 Muséum
National d'Histoire Naturelle

 Gardens free; Grande
Serre €2.30; Ménagerie
€5 ages 17 and up,
€3.50 children 4–16

Gardens daily 7:30–sunset; Ménagerie
June–Sept, M–Sa 9–6, Su 9–6:30;
Oct–May, M–Sa 9–5, Su 9–6:30

All ages

in 1794. Kids can see bears, giraffes, lions, orangutans, dozens of monkeys and birds, a variety of snakes, and even a few giant turtles. All the animals look well cared for, but their cages are small. This means kids can get a close-up look at them, but the animals themselves look bored and unhappy. At the Microzoo (for kids 10 and up), within the main zoo, kids can use microscopes to check out microscopic animal life, including all the little creatures that live on a piece of cheese (not recommended just before lunch).

Nature-loving kids like checking out a tree that's supposedly the oldest in Paris, a faux acacia planted in 1636; it's on the allée de Becquerel. The Grande Serre (Great Greenhouse) nearby is so full of hothouse plants gone wild that going inside it is like a trip to the tropics (warning: it's closed Tuesdays). Kids can climb on the big rock at the back of the greenhouse to get a great view of this real urban jungle.

KEEP IN MIND Kids *really* interested in plants will like the École de Botanique, with thousands of rare plants, and the Jardin Alpin, with plants from mountainous regions all over the world. Both these gardens are within the main garden near the zoo. Note that the Jardin des Plantes is not always clean, especially in the woodsy section by the maze.

JARDIN DES TUILERIES

Thanks to its wide gravel walks, placid fountains, lawns—all with *pelouse interdite* (keep off the grass) signs—and carefully manicured flower beds stretching between the Louvre and the place de la Concorde, the Jardin des Tuileries is without a doubt the city's most elegant park. For generations, Parisian families have come here for outings. Parents relax on park benches while kids run around or, best of all, sail little boats on one of the park's ponds. (You rent a boat and a long pole from a stand next to the pond, hope your kids' boat will be one of the ones whose sails catch the wind, and encourage your children to use the pole to prod their craft away from the side of the pond if it gets stuck.)

This formal park had very humble beginnings: In the 15th century it was a quarry for clay that was used in making *tuiles* (roof tiles), the source of the park's name. Marie de Medici had the idea of creating an elegant, Italian-style garden here, and later André

EATS FOR KIDS There are **snack bars** and **drinks stands** scattered around the Tuileries. **Café Véry** (tel. 01–47–03–94–84)—chic, reasonably priced, and right in the middle of the park—has a good kids' menu and inventive light meals. You can also come here just for a pastry and sit indoors or out. **Angelina** (226 rue de Rivoli, tel. 01–42--60–82-00), a tearoom founded in 1903, serves to-die-for hot chocolate and excellent (though pricey) pastries; kids must be on their best behavior. You'll see some very well-dressed Parisian families here. See also Musée du Louvre and Jardins du Palais-Royal.

Between pl. de la Concorde and the Louvre, 1er. Métro: Tuileries, Louvre

 Free

01-40-20-90-43

Apr–June and Sept, daily 7 AM–9 PM; July–Aug, M–F 7 AM–11:45 PM, Sa–Su 7 AM–1:45 AM; Oct–Mar, daily 7 AM–7:30 PM

All ages

Le Nôtre, the great 17th-century garden designer responsible for the park around the Château de Versailles, embellished the park.

Today, the Tuileries contains many attractions for kids. A spacious, shady kids' play area has a sandbox and climbing equipment, a merry-go-round, sleepy little ponies to ride (though this tends to bore anyone over 7, since the ponies are led in a group), a Guignol puppet theater, special paths for skateboarders and rollerbladers, a trampoline, and even an open-air ice-skating rink in winter. In July and August and at Christmas, an enormous, garish carnival rises on the site, complete with a zillion stands where you can try your luck at various games, a roller-coaster ride, and a huge—REALLY huge—Ferris wheel. Kids love it, but it's a good thing Marie de Medici and Le Nôtre aren't around to see this.

KEEP IN MIND
You can rent the little sailboats on Wednesdays, weekends, and school holidays. An association called L'Enfance de l'Art (tel. 01–42–96–19–33) organizes excellent 90-minute workshops in art and gardening (in French) for kids 4–12 in the Tuileries.

HEY, KIDS! The Tuileries has seen a lot of world firsts: the first public toilets (in the 18th century), the first newspaper stand, and the first flight of a hot-air balloon, a 20-minute trip above Paris made by the Montgolfier brothers in 1783. Just a few years after that, in 1791, King Louis XVI and Marie-Antoinette tried to escape revolutionary mobs by fleeing across the Tuileries, but they were caught and thrown into prison and later guillotined on the nearby place de la Concorde.

JARDIN DU LUXEMBOURG

This oh-so-Parisian park, the city's favorite for generations, has it all: a beautiful palace, designed in 1615 and now the home of the French Sénat; huge trees; ponies to ride; tennis courts; beehives; the Grand Bassin pond, where kids can sail boats; and even—rarest of all in Paris—an area where you can actually walk on the grass (if you're accompanied by a toddler). One of the park's treasures is its merry-go-round, whose much-loved wooden animals were designed by none other than Charles Garnier, the 19th-century architect of the Paris Opéra. Next to the merry-go-round is the park's own puppet theater, the city's biggest (see Marionnettes du Luxembourg).

You'll find a special fenced-in kids' play area with its own admission charge in the southwest corner of the park, next to the puppet theater. It's kept spotlessly clean (not always the case in Paris parks) and filled with all sorts of structures kids can climb on, swing down,

KEEP IN MIND If you take the kids to the fenced-in play area (highly recommended) and want to leave it—to see a puppet show, for example—but come back later, be sure to get your hands stamped at the desk on your way out.

EATS FOR KIDS In the park's center, **La Buvette des Marionnettes du Luxembourg** (tel. 01-43-26-33-04) serves drinks, sandwiches, salads, crêpes, and ice cream, and there are tables outside under the chestnut trees. If your kids just have to have American-style burgers, look for the **McDonald's** (65 bd. St-Michel, tel. 01-46-33-02-08) nearby. For a special splurge on Sunday, head to **Hôtel Méridien Montparnasse** (19 rue du Commandant-Mouchotte, tel. 01-44-36-44-00) for the "Baby Brunch," with sumptuous kids' and adults' buffets and entertainment for kids (€38.50 ages 13 and up, €17 ages 4–12).

Entrances: rue de Medicis, rue Guynemer, bd.
St-Michel, rue de Vaugirard, 6e. Métro: Odéon.
RER: Luxembourg

08–36–68–31–12; Office de Tourisme
www.paris-bienvenue.com

 Free, some
attractions charge

Apr–Oct, daily 7–sunset;
Nov–Mar, daily 8–sunset

All ages

swirl through the air on, or simply sit in. Toddlers head to the sandbox, and bigger kids with an urge to climb gravitate toward a tall spider-web contraption that looks a little like the Eiffel Tower.

Chess players congregate in front of the glass-walled Orangerie, which has a free play area for small children in front of it. In the middle of the park, you'll find some placid ponies that take little kids for a short ride. Children in the mood for more action like the pedal-powered cars that operate near the park's southern edge. You can join the joggers along a popular circuit around the park, toss bits of baguette to resident pigeons, or, best of all, sit down in one of the park's distinctive pale-green metal chairs, listen to Parisians chattering around you, and realize you're really, truly in Paris.

HEY, KIDS! If you want to try your luck catching brass rings on the merry-go-round, choose a mount in the outer circle of animals (the ones closest to the edge). An attendant will hand you a stick. As the merry-go-round begins to turn, try to get your stick through the middle of the ring hanging down from a post. If you do it right (hint: keep the stick straight), the ring will fall off onto your stick, and the attendant will put a new ring on the post for the next child. After the ride, you give your rings back.

JARDINS DU PALAIS-ROYAL

The Jardins du Palais-Royal (actually a single park, although the name is plural) is one of Paris's best-kept secrets, even though it's right in the middle of the most touristed part of the city, just a short walk from the Louvre. Almost always overlooked by visitors, this lovely little park surrounded by elegant 18th-century buildings (the writer Colette lived in one of them) is hard to find. You get to it by going through small passageways that you could walk right past and not see.

The park has long gravel walkways, shady trees, magnificently planted flower beds, lots of park benches, and—most special of all—hardly any traffic noise, because the buildings all around it block out the sound of the cars roaring by just a few yards away. Although it looks very formal, the park is popular among Parisian families, especially ones with smaller kids, since they can run around safe from traffic.

Toddlers can practice taking steps from park bench to park bench or play in the sandbox

Entrances: off pl. André-Malraux, rue Beaujolais, rue de Valois, 1er. Métro: Palais-Royal

 Free

 Apr–May and Sept, daily 7:30 AM–10 PM; June–Aug, daily 7:30 AM–11 PM; Oct–Mar, daily 7:30 AM–8:30 PM

08-36-68-31-12 Office de Tourisme; www.paris-bienvenue.com

All ages

at the north end of the park, while bigger kids can kick a soccer ball or just play around on the artworks at the south end of the park. One of these, an installation by architect Daniel Buren, caused a controversy when it was built—its contemporary style contrasts sharply with the 18th-century structures around it—but kids love it. The installation is a wide expanse of pavement with water flowing under it, visible through grids. Punctuating it are a series of columns kids can climb on and rows of little red lights in the pavement that make it look like a miniature landing strip. Don't forget to toss a coin into the pool near the columns and make a wish—it's a Paris tradition. Among the other public art here is a fountain with shiny silver balls, created by Pol Bury. In a flat, paved area around the fountain, little kids practice their roller-skating skills and supremely talented skateboarders sometimes show off their stuff. Kids might not know it's art, but they know they like it.

KEEP IN MIND
La Boutique du Palais-Royal (9 rue Beaujolais, tel. 01–42–60–08–22), one of the elegant shops under the surrounding arcades, sells handmade wooden toys and other creative treats for kids. The astronomically priced toy soldiers in the antiques stores here are strictly for collectors.

HEY, KIDS! If you're in this park at noon on Saturday, don't be surprised if you hear a loud BOOM. It's the Palais-Royal cannon. This little cannon, in a flower bed near the south end of the park, boomed at noon every day from 1786 to 1914—at least, when there was enough sun. The heat of sun shining through a magnifying glass at a precise angle activated the firing mechanism so that it would set off a small charge of gunpowder precisely at midday. Today, the firing mechanism is automatic.

MARIONNETTES DU LUXEMBOURG

Puppet theaters abound throughout Paris, but the city's biggest is ideally located in the middle of the Jardin du Luxembourg (see #39). It's the Marionnettes du Luxembourg, and the classic puppet shows staged here are bound to please your kids whether or not they speak French.

Opened in 1933 by the Desarthis family and still run by them, the puppet theater occupies a nondescript building in the middle of the park, next to the merry-go-round and near the fenced-in play area. Before each show, staff members ring a bell outside the theater to let you know it's time to stand in line.

The shows change regularly, but all feature the classic French puppet hero Guignol, who has been around since at least the 18th century, when he was cast as a bloodthirsty villain. Today, Guignol is definitely the good guy. He's the character with a long black pigtail

HEY, KIDS!

When you enter the theater, leave your parents behind and go sit as close to the stage as possible to get a good look at the action (and the puppets, which are bigger than you might think). The front rows are for kids only.

KEEP IN MIND Other good Parisian puppet theaters are the Guignol du Jardin d'Acclimatation, in the Bois de Boulogne (16e); the Marionnettes du Champ de Mars, near the Eiffel Tower (7e); the Marionnettes des Champs-Élysées, in the Jardin des Champs-Élysées (8e); the Guignol de Paris, in the Parc des Buttes Chaumont (19e); and the Marionnettes du Parc Georges Brassens (15e). Performances at all of them are given on Wednesday, Saturday, and Sunday afternoons and more often during school vacations. See individual listings for several of these parks.

Jardin du Luxembourg, 6e. Métro: Odéon. RER: Luxembourg

 €4

 01–43–26–46–47

 W, Sa–Su, and school holidays at 3 (sometimes 2 shows)

4 and up

wearing a long Chinese-style coat, but you won't have to look for him, because as soon as he appears on stage every French kid in the audience will shriek his name. Guignol has a good heart but is constantly getting into trouble, usually by trying to help out one of his neighbors in the generic French village (or Paris neighborhood) where he lives. As Guignol stumbles blindly into one disaster after another, kids scream advice to him, warn him about the bad guys, and in general try to help him, but no matter what they do, Guignol is bound to get his head whacked more than once. Your children should have no problem getting the gist of the story. At intermission, the curtain closes and kids crowd around the front of the stage, where nice ladies sell candy.

Thankfully, Guignol always manages to emerge unscathed, and at the end of each show, he takes a few bows and tells the audience to come back again soon. Your kids will no doubt be happy to do just that.

EATS FOR KIDS **Pâtisserie Dalloyau** (2 pl. Edmund-Rostand, tel. 01–43–29–31–10) sells delicious pastries as well as quiches and sandwiches that you can take out or sample in the store's elegant in-house tearoom. Well-dressed Parisian moms and grandmothers bring their equally well-dressed, well-behaved children here for a treat after a stroll in the park. The casual **La Buvette des Marionnettes du Luxembourg** (tel. 01–43–26–33–04), next to the theater, has drinks, snacks, light meals, and ice cream. See also Jardin du Luxembourg.

MÉDAILLONS D'ARAGO

Paris is filled with monuments to France's native sons and daughters, but there's one you could easily miss. In fact, you could step on it and not see it, and finding it is a treasure hunt kids should enjoy. The monument honors Dominique Arago (1786–1853), an astronomer and physicist who made major contributions to the early study of electromagnetism and who patriotically championed the Paris meridian (the longitude line that passes through the city) as the international mean-time line. France and Ireland actually kept to French mean time until 1911, when both countries joined the world in adopting Greenwich mean time.

In honor of Arago's achievements, France erected a bronze statue of him that once stood on the boulevard Arago (also named for him), but the German army melted the statue down during World War II. Then in 1995 Arago was again honored, this time with a most unusual monument: a series of 135 bronze *médaillons* (disks)—each 12 centimeters (4½ inches) in diameter and marked simply with the name Arago—implanted in pavement several meters

EATS FOR KIDS Near the observatory, the bistro **Contre-Allée** (83 av. Denfert-Rochereau, tel. 01–43–54–99–86) prepares generous servings of classic French cooking, though it's not cheap. Restaurants and food shops line colorful rue Daguerre, including **Le Moulin de la Vièrge** (82 rue Daguerre, tel. 01–53–91–52–10), for delicious breads (try the sourdough *pain au levain*) and pastries. See also Catacombes and Jardin du Luxembourg. If you're hunting on the quai Malaquais, look under the Musée d'Orsay for suggestions, or take along a picnic to share with the ducks that hang out on the quai.

Sq. Ile de Seine, 98 bd. Arago, 14e to Montmartre library, 18 av. Pte-de-Montmartre, 18e. Métro: Denfert-Rochereau, St-Jacques, Porte de Clignancourt

08–36–68–31–12 Office de Tourisme; www.paris-bienvenue.com

 Free

 Daily 24 hrs

4 and up

apart along the Paris meridian line. The line of disks (some of which have been stolen) begins where the Arago statue once stood, on the boulevard Arago facing the gardens of the Observatoire de Paris (Paris Observatory).

The line passes through the Jardin du Luxembourg, the quai Malaquais, the Jardin des Tuileries, and the Jardins du Palais-Royal (see listings) before ending on the city's northern edge, in front of the Bibliothèque de la Porte de Montmartre (Montmartre's public library). The observatory, where Arago once worked, has been a center for the study of time and the stars since it was built in 1667. Its south wall is on Paris's latitude line (48°50'), and the Paris meridian passes right through it, so naturally a few Arago disks are in the observatory and its garden (observatory closed to visitors; garden open May–October). To go on a treasure hunt, start in the square Ile de Seine, in the observatory garden, or anywhere along the Paris meridian, and look out for Arago under your feet.

HEY, KIDS! One good spot to find Arago is on the quai Malaquais (métro: St-Germain-des-Prés), across the Seine from the Louvre. Walk west along the quai from where the Passerelle des Arts pedestrian bridge meets the Left Bank, keeping your eyes peeled for a disk.

KEEP IN MIND The detailed Institut Géographique National (IGN) map of Paris, sold at most Paris bookstores and *maisons de presse* (newspaper shops), shows the meridian line. If you search for Arago on the quai Malaquais, remember that Paris quais do not have barriers along the Seine. Keep the kids away from the edge!

MUSÉE DE LA CONTREFAÇON

Will the real Barbie please stand up? That may be the only way you can figure out which one she is, without the help of this quirky little museum devoted to exposing trickery. Its name means the Museum of Counterfeits, and it exhibits fake Hermès scarves, fake Louis Vuitton bags with the famous "LV" logo, and, more interesting to kids, fake Legos, fake computer games, fake running shoes, and lots of fake toys, all displayed next to genuine originals. You'll see about 400 items in all, proof that nothing is safe from the counterfeiter.

The counterfeits here really do run the gamut. A bunch of Barbie dolls look almost exactly, but not quite, like a real Barbie, and a coffeemaker *does* look exactly like the real thing, only with a different brand name. Some fakes look pretty, well, fakey, while others resemble the originals so closely that you can understand how so many people get taken in by high-priced counterfeit goods every year. That's why the Union des Fabricants, a

KEEP IN MIND This museum could make a fun side trip from the nearby Bois de Boulogne (see #63), especially since the entrance fee is so low. It's also a nice excuse for a little French lesson: "counterfeit" comes from the French words *contre* ("against") and *fait* ("made").

EATS FOR KIDS Head to **Pâtisserie Alsacienne** (91 av. Raymond-Poincaré, tel. 01–45–00–56–55) for yummy quiches, *kougelhopf* (brioche-type bread with candied fruits), strudel, and *gâteau forêt-noire* (Black Forest cake). **Lillo** (35 rue des Belles-Feuilles, tel. 01–47–27–69–08) is one of Paris's top cheese stores. Try the kid-pleasing *comté* or various take-out items made with cheese, like *gougères* (cheesy cream puffs) or the *feuilleté de roquefort* (cheese-filled puff pastry). Reliable **Bistro Romain** (6 pl. Victor-Hugo, tel. 01–45–00–65–03) has a good kids' menu (lasagna or hamburger and fries) and all-you-can-eat chocolate mousse. See also Bois de Boulogne.

16 rue de la Faisanderie,
16e. Métro: Porte Dauphine

 01-56-26-14-00; www.unifab.com

 €2.30 ages 12 and up

 T-Su 2-5:30

10 and up

French manufacturer's organization, set up this museum: to show people how widespread counterfeiting is and what problems it can cause. One display shows how counterfeits can rip off both the original producer of an item and the consumer, who might get an inferior product. Another demonstrates how fake toys, appliances, and industrial parts can actually be very dangerous, and yet another reveals that cheap counterfeit goods bought abroad may turn out not to be a bargain after all, since savvy customs officials often confiscate them. Historical objects, such as a counterfeit Gallo-Roman amphora created centuries ago (and donated to the museum by Jacques Cousteau), show that counterfeiting has been around for a very long time.

There's nothing hands-on in this museum, but kids should have fun trying to pick out the details that make the fakes different from the real things. Older kids are usually intrigued by the moral issues of counterfeiting that this museum brings to their attention.

HEY, KIDS! Things aren't always what they seem, and one such thing is the building this museum is in. It looks just like an 18th-century Parisian town-house, but it isn't. It was built in authentic 18th-century style, all right, but the house was built a century later, in the late 19th century, in imitation of a certain 18th-century mansion in the Marais district, on the other side of town. That mansion has since been torn down, but this fake is still here. The moral of the story: sometimes fakes outlive the originals.

MUSÉE DE LA CURIOSITÉ ET DE LA MAGIE

Any kid (or grown-up) who has ever tried to perform magic tricks is bound to be enthralled by this very unusual museum housed in centuries-old vaulted cellars in the heart of the ancient Marais district. Visitors set out on a journey into the world of illusion, their senses on the alert as they try to separate truth from falsehood. It's not easy. You see strange animated objects, test your perceptions with interactive optical illusions, learn the secrets of bizarre scientific equipment, and check out various tools of the magician's trade. The really original feature of this museum is that its staff members are all trained magicians. They act as your guides throughout your visit, performing magic tricks to show you their craft in action.

This is museum as performance space, and audience participation is part of the show. You see conjuring tricks, sleight-of-hand card tricks, and other thought-teasers that have attracted audiences to magic shows for centuries. The museum's exhibits also give you a

EATS FOR KIDS **Le Loir dans la Théière** (3 rue des Rosiers, tel. 01–42–72–68–12), a tearoom, serves scrumptious snacks in an Alice-in-Wonderland atmosphere. For delicious U.S. and U.S.-style treats, try **Thanksgiving** (20 rue St-Paul, tel. 01–42–77–68–29), a combination restaurant and take-out shop. Friendly **Le Petit Bofinger** (6 rue de la Bastille, tel. 01–42–72–05–23), a bistro branch of a chic brasserie, has good fixed-price menus. For picnic goods, check out the food shops on the rue St-Antoine. For breads, don't miss the *baguette à l'ancienne* or the olive *fougasse* at **Malineau** (26 rue St-Paul, tel. 01–43–54–97–15). See also Musée Picasso and Place des Vosges and the Marais.

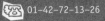

history of magic from ancient times to the present. Everything is in French, but staff members are usually able to make explanations in English, if necessary; gestures can go a long way, too. The enthusiastic guides are very good at getting kids involved in the act and try to give every child a chance to participate at some point. You're also given time to conduct your own experiments with the interactive equipment.

On Saturdays the museum operates the École de Magie (School of Magic), open to anyone 12 or older, adults included, with separate classes for advanced students (2–3 PM) and beginners (3:15–4 PM). All classes are in French. The whole family can learn how to wow friends back home with feats of illusion. Afternoon-long Ateliers Magiques (Magic Classes, held in French) that include a guided visit of the museum, lessons in performing magic tricks, a snack, and a show for parents are organized for kids 7–12 during school holidays.

HEY, KIDS! Have you ever heard of the English expression "legerdemain"? It comes from the French words for "light" (*leger*), "of" (*de*), and "hand" (*main*), or in other words, sleight-of-hand. The French don't use this expression, though. When they mean "legerdemain," they say *prestidigitation*. Go figure!

KEEP IN MIND The École de Magie is a popular family activity, so it's best to check opening times and reserve in advance if you'd like to participate. After your visit to the museum, you might want to take a look at the nearby Magasin de Magie store (13 rue du Temple, tel. 01-42-74-06-74). Here you can stock up on magic wands, boxes with secret compartments, decks of trick cards, and even videos (in French) showing you how to perform various magic tricks.

MUSÉE DE LA POUPÉE

The doll lovers in your family won't want to miss this small museum. Hidden away on a tiny dead-end street and with a minuscule front garden, the museum is the perfect home for the more than 500 dolls on display, most of them produced in France from 1800 to 2000. You'll see examples of all sorts of dolls made out of all sorts of materials, from porcelain and papier-mâché to rubber and plastic.

Beyond the displays of dolls, this museum gives you a history of the doll in France since the beginning of the 19th century. From 1800 to 1870, for example, French dolls represented women and came complete with elaborate outfits that would put Barbie to shame, but a doll exhibit at the Paris world's fair of 1878 started a new trend of dolls in the form of babies and kids. From playing with dolls meant to look like *maman*, little French girls began to play at being *maman* themselves, and the museum's collection shows you this evolution in hundreds of examples.

HEY, KIDS!

Bleuette, an early-20th-century equivalent of Barbie, came with a lot more clothes than most kids have in their closets. Very industrious owners could sew more outfits for Bleuette using patterns. Get a good look at Bleuette in Room 3, and imagine trying to climb a tree in clothes like these.

KEEP IN MIND The dead-end street on which the museum is located is tricky to find; it begins near 22 rue Rambuteau. This museum would make a good side trip on the day you visit the nearby Centre National d'Art et de Culture Georges Pompidou (see #58). If your family has divided opinions on doll museums, some of you—accompanied by a parent—can run around on the square in front of the Pompidou center or check out the Tinguely–Saint Phalle fountain while others visit the Musée de la Poupée.

Impasse Berthaud,
3e. Métro: Rambuteau

  €6 adults, €4 ages
19–25, €3 children 3–18

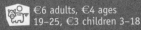 T–Su 10–6

 7 and up

01–42–72–73–11

The elaborate settings in which the dolls are presented provide a visual overview of fashions and domestic life in France since the early 19th century and should interest even non-doll-fans. Fashion lovers can check out what a well-dressed *Parisienne* would have been wearing in around 1810, see a variety of regional costumes, or get a close look at 1950s styles through several dolls that a French fashion magazine originally sold. Younger kids should enjoy seeing the kinds of clothes children once wore and the tiny toys in several displays that show what French kids have played with over the years.

The Musée de la Poupée includes a doll clinic where you can bring dolls to be repaired; collectors can purchase rare (and very expensive) dolls as well as parts to be used in restoring antique dolls. At the small shop you can buy dolls, doll clothes, and doll furniture. Don't miss the tiny copper pans that no French doll kitchen should ever be without.

EATS FOR KIDS Tiny **Le Potager du Marais** (22 rue Rambuteau, tel. 01–44–54–00–31), around the corner from the doll museum, prepares tasty dishes made with organic ingredients. You'll find soups, salads, quiches, and special treats like warm goat cheese and honey on whole-wheat bread, as well as main courses using organic poultry and naturally raised fish. See also Centre National d'Art et de Culture Georges Pompidou, Musée Picasso, and Musée des Arts et Métiers.

MUSÉE DE L'AIR ET DE L'ESPACE

For anyone who loves airplanes, this air and space museum is a must. It's in the historic Aéroport Le Bourget, the former main city airport. If the name sounds familiar, that's because aviator Charles Lindbergh landed his *Spirit of St. Louis* here in May 1927, becoming the first person to complete a transatlantic flight. What you may not know is that 13 days earlier, pilots Charles Nungesser and François Coli took off from Le Bourget in an attempt to do the same—but disappeared. You can learn about their flight and other aviation history at this vast exhibition space, which occupies the former main terminal and part of a runway and showcases air travel from 1879 to the present.

The Prototypes 1945–1970 et l'Armée de l'Air exhibit contains prototypes and military aircraft, and Entre Deux Guerres displays light aircraft and stunt planes from 1920 to 1970, with a concentration on nonmilitary aircraft from the 1920s and 1930s (the period between the two world wars that the exhibit name implies). The Hall de l'Espace has models of satellites, including *Sputnik 57*, and of *Apollo 13,* and in the Hall Concorde you can climb aboard the

KEEP IN MIND Kids who aren't thrilled by airplanes, as well as younger children (6 and under), may soon tire of viewing plane after plane in vast hangars and exhibition spaces, especially since there's a lot of walking involved. If you think that might be a problem, limit your visit to the top kid-pleasers: the Grande Galerie, where the rarest and earliest aircraft are displayed, and the Hall Concorde, where kids can get inside a Concorde. In mid-June in odd-numbered years, Le Bourget airport hosts the huge Paris air show (official name: Salon Internationale de l'Aéronautique et de l'Espace).

Aéroport Le Bourget, Le Bourget

 €6 ages 17 and up, €4.50 children 8–16

May–Oct, T–Su 10–6; Nov–Apr, T–Su 10–5

 01–49–92–71–99; www.mae.org

7 and up

prototype for the first Concorde and see famous planes flown during World War II, such as the Spitfire and Mustang.

The Grande Galerie includes aviation instruments and equipment from the earliest days of flying machines, along with a superb collection of early aircraft (1879–1918). You can see the passenger section of the 1884 *La France* dirigible, a 1906 Vuia plane, and Henri Fabre's 1910 *hydraplane*. Looking at these tiny, fragile-looking constructions makes you appreciate the courage of early aviators. Outside on the runway, you can check out combat planes, rocket launchers, two Ariane rockets, a Boeing 747, and a Concorde. The 3-D film shown in a little movie theater next to the Ariane rockets is usually a hit with kids.

To help kids get the most out of their visit, the museum has prepared brochures (in French) that use stories to guide you through the collection.

EATS FOR KIDS
You can try the café in the air-port, **Eurobar** (tel. 01–48–35–92–70), but a better bet is **Le Wagon-Le Rail d'Ouesssant** (15 bis rue Jean-Moulin, in nearby St-Denis, tel. 01–48–23–23–41), where the waiters and kitchen staff, all students at a restaurant school, will usually make up special kids' meals on request (open weekdays for lunch only).

GETTING HERE By car or taxi, take the A1 highway north of Paris to the Aérogare Le Bourget exit (around 8 kilometers/5 miles). By public transport, take the métro to the La Courneuve–8 Mai stop, or take the RER commuter train (line B) from the center of Paris to Le Bourget, which is a stop on the train to Aéro-port Roissy-Charles-de-Gaulle. From outside the entrance of either the métro or the RER station, take the number 152 bus to Aérogare Le Bourget. The trip by public transportation should take around 30 minutes, depending on train and bus connections.

MUSÉE DES ARTS ET MÉTIERS

The Musée des Arts et Métiers (Arts and Crafts Museum) would be better called the Museum of Inventions. Why? Because it doesn't showcase arts and crafts at all, but rather all sorts of technical innovations made from the 16th century to our own day. It's a place of inspiration for the world's next Leonardo da Vincis, and those who nurture and admire them.

The museum occupies a spectacular building: the medieval abbey of St-Martin-des-Champs, completely renovated for the 21st century. Containing over 80,000 objects and documents, it illustrates groundbreaking, world-changing discoveries in the fields of physics, optics, mechanics, telecommunications, and more. Among these testaments to human creativity are everything from weird 18th-century versions of robots to the first movie cameras, invented by brothers Auguste-Marie and Louis-Jean Lumière in the late 19th century. One of the museum's prize objects—displayed in the abbey's former chapel,

KEEP IN MIND Although this museum is much less hands-on than other Paris museums dedicated to scientific accomplishments, the over-7 crowd should still love looking at the planes, the pendulum, and other strange objects. There's an audio guide in English, and classes on technical skills like engraving are given for kids 7–12 (in French).

HEY, KIDS! *Star Wars* would never have been possible without the Lumière brothers (or someone like them). These aptly named men (*lumière* means "light") invented the world's first movie camera, made the world's first movies, and opened the world's first movie theater. Their first film wouldn't win an Academy Award; it only showed workers leaving their factory. However, the second one, *L'Arroseur Arrosé* (*The Waterer Gets Watered*), could still make you laugh. The first-ever fiction film, it's not as impressive as a *Skywalker* saga, but hey, it was made more than a century ago.

292 rue St-Martin, 3e. Métro: Arts-et-Métiers

01–53–01–82–00; www.arts-et-metiers.net

 €5.50 ages 19 and up, €3.80 ages 5–18

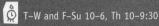 T–W and F–Su 10–6, Th 10–9:30

7 and up

just to show you where this museum's heart is—is a little 24-horsepower monoplane built by the French inventor and flyer Louis Blériot. He used it to become the first person to fly over the English Channel, in 1909.

Items from the 20th century include some equipment with which kids can do their own experiments with sound. (Although some exhibits are interactive, other science-oriented museums in Paris have more of these.) The museum's most stunning object is without a doubt the two-story pendulum created by the French physicist Jean-Bernard-Léon Foucault (1819–1868). Among his many inventions, which included the gyroscope and the first polarizer, Foucault used a pendulum to demonstrate that the earth rotates once a day. As Foucault's huge pendulum swings silently back and forth in a vast room, seemingly operated by unseen giants, it gives kids graphic proof that we are really swirling around in space.

EATS FOR KIDS A nearby spot for a park-bench picnic, the shady square du Temple also has a kids' play area. **Léon de Bruxelles** (8 pl. de la République, tel. 01–43–38–25–19), a chain famous for its mussels, has one of the cheapest kids' menus in Paris, along with good fries. (Don't worry: you can choose a hamburger instead of mussels.) **À la Mexicaine** (68 rue Quincampoix, tel. 01–48–87–99–34) specializes in Mexican (not Tex-Mex) dishes like *mole poblano* (stew with chocolate in the sauce) and homemade tortillas; it has a good kids' menu.

MUSÉE D'ORSAY

The vast Musée d'Orsay, a turn-of-the-20th-century railway station imaginatively redesigned by architect Gae Aulenti, still bears marks of its past life, such as the great clock on the Seine-facing facade. (Inside the museum, kids like checking out the clock's workings from the back.) The museum showcases works created from 1848 to 1914, when Paris was recognized as the world's arts capital. Parents may come for the Impressionist paintings, but kids like the variety of objects—from tiny, very early photographs of Paris to gigantic sculptures—presented in a high-ceilinged space with lots of elbow room.

The Musée d'Orsay deserves kudos for making its collection accessible to younger visitors. Pick up a free art-quiz pamphlet, "Carnets Parcours Familles" (available in English), when you enter the museum, and organize your own museum visit in the form of a game. The museum also organizes special 90-minute guided tours for kids ages 5–10 and their families, and other tours just for kids, in which guides bring the collection to life through stories, games, and other activities. These are usually in French, but some guides can translate

EATS FOR KIDS The museum's **Café des Hauteurs** under the giant clock serves snacks and light dishes cafeteria-style except during lunch and dinner hours, when it can get extremely crowded. An elegant (and more expensive) alternative is the **Restaurant du Musée d'Orsay** on the museum's second level. On Sunday mornings, an **organic food market** on the boulevard Raspail (métro: Sèvres–Babylone) has great picnic finds, including crêpes and hot U.S.-style muffins. For park benches, try the little square des Missions Étrangères off the rue du Bac or the square Boucicault near the Sèvres–Babylone métro; both have kids' play areas.

1 rue de la Légion d'Honneur, 7e. Métro: Assemblée Nationale

 01-45-49-48-14 or 01-45-49-11-11; www.musee-orsay.fr

 €7 adults 26 and up (Su €5), €5 ages 18–25, ages 17 and under free

Oct–mid-June, T–W and F–Sa 10–6, Th 10–9:45, Su 9–6; mid-June–Sept, T–W and F–Sa 9–6, Th 9–9:45, Su 9–6

 6 and up

into English. Showings of early silent films, accompanied by a real piano player, and concerts of turn-of-the-20th-century music are other activities at the museum for kids and their families.

In addition to lush Rodin sculptures, early movie posters, decorative art, and rare examples of early photography, the Musée d'Orsay displays works by some of France's greatest painters (Delacroix, Ingres, and others). Favorites among many visitors are works by Impressionists and post-Impressionists, grouped on the museum's upper level. Along with paintings by Monet, Manet, Cézanne, Sisley, Pissarro, and Renoir, you find Dégas's sculpture *Petite danseuse de quatorze ans* (*Little 14-Year-Old Dancer*), a model for budding ballerinas. Families planning a visit to Monet's house at Giverny, west of Paris (see Fondation Claude Monet), should definitely check out the artist's paintings displayed here, such as *Coquelicots* (*Poppies*), with its bright red blossoms.

HEY, KIDS! Want to feel like Mary Poppins, French-style? A glass floor lets you walk above the scale model of the Opéra neighborhood. The Opéra was *the* place to see and be seen in late 19th-century Paris, the period when most of the museum's works were created.

KEEP IN MIND If you arrive with a baby in a backpack or in a large stroller, you'll be asked to check it (the pack or stroller, not the baby) at the main desk. The museum lends folding strollers, though. For additional information about special family-oriented museum visits and activities, go to the Espace Jeunes (Youth Desk) on the museum's basement level or call 01-40-49-48-48. You can make reservations here (recommended) for guided tours, film screenings, and concerts.

MUSÉE DU LOUVRE

Just because the world's most famous museum is filled with priceless treasures that include Leonardo da Vinci's *Mona Lisa* and the *Venus de Milo* doesn't mean that kids will like it. The sheer size of this former palace makes it overwhelming for everyone, children especially. But that doesn't mean you should avoid it either. Your best strategy is to think of the Louvre as a long-term project, and plan to see only a small part of it each time you come. Pick up a free map at the museum's entrance and narrow your visit down to a few key areas. The useful "First Visit" brochure, in English, lists 50 top works of art and where to find them, although 50 is still too many for most kids.

The basic organization of the Louvre is actually simple, with three main wings—Richelieu, Sully, and Denon. Of the three, Sully is probably your best bet with youngsters, because it's the wing with the mummies and other Egyptian artifacts. You can see sarcophagi, papyrus, and mummies of all sorts—people, cats, even fish—all wrapped up in their

KEEP IN MIND The museum's rue de Rivoli entrance usually has shorter lines. Come to the Louvre at night to see its stunning exterior artfully lit. The Louvre organizes excellent guided tours and workshops for kids (in French); call 01–40–20–52–09 for subjects and times.

HEY, KIDS! Hieroglyphics—the ancient Egyptian form of writing that uses pictures of objects to represent sounds and words—were a mystery until a French specialist on Egypt, Jean-Francois Champollion, figured them out in 1822. Five years later, he set up the Egyptian section of the Louvre. Check out the hieroglyphics on the *Palette au nom du roi Toutankhamon (Tablet in the Name of King Tutankhamen)* in the Civilisation Pharaonique (Civilization of the Pharaohs) room. It's a wooden tablet with sea-grass pens and ink holders from King Tut's day (around 1336–1327 BC). Imagine having to do your homework on something like this.

34–36 quai du Louvre and
99 rue de Rivoli, 1er. Métro: Louvre

 01-40-20-53-17, 01-40-20-51-51
in English; www.louvre.fr

 €7.50 adults 18
and up, after
3 and Su €5, 1st
Su of month free

 Th–Su 9–6 (Richelieu Wing M to
9:45), M and W 9–9:45

7 and up

creepy bandages. Kids should like the incredibly realistic statue known as the *Seated Scribe*, which dates from the time of the Great Pyramids. You'll also find intricate Roman mosaics and Etruscan art, along with the Greek masterpieces the *Venus de Milo* and the *Winged Victory of Samothrace*.

The Denon Wing has paintings from the Italian Renaissance, and that means the *Mona Lisa,* which is sealed up under glass and always surrounded by worshipers. The only way for kids to get even a glimpse of the famous smile is to nudge their way through the crowd. The Denon Wing also includes the grandiose Galerie d'Apollon, which has a potential kid-pleaser, King Louis XV's jewel-encrusted crown. Outside the Louvre, the I. M. Pei pyramid over the museum's main entrance is surrounded by fountains and a wide paved area where kids can run around.

EATS FOR KIDS Under the museum in the chic Carrousel du Louvre shopping mall, the self-service **Universal Resto** (tel. 01–47–03–96–58) is a huge food hall with fresh, reasonably priced food representing 12 different cuisines, from Lebanese to Tex-Mex. Trendy **Le Marly** (Palais du Louvre, 93 rue de Rivoli, tel. 01–49–26–06–60), a café overlooking the pyramid, isn't cheap by any means, but the view of the pyramid is one-of-a-kind. The most affordable option is to come here for afternoon coffee and pastry, as long as you're not in a hurry. See also Jardin des Tuileries and Jardins du Palais-Royal.

MUSÉE EN HERBE

I f your kids say they hate museums, bring them here and prove them wrong. Paris's first museum just for children (*en herbe* means "young sprouts," as in kids) believes that the best way for youngsters to learn is to have fun and move around. Almost everything on display is meant to be touched, fiddled with, or laughed at, and children don't just walk through exhibits; they're given a treasure map that guides them on a quest. While small kids manipulate geometric objects in kid-friendly colors and sizes, bigger kids can create art on their own faces using the makeup that's always on hand.

Most permanent exhibits have to do with the arts—interactive displays illustrating perspective or color combinations, for example—but the innovative temporary exhibits (changing every six months or so) broaden the focus to include cultural topics, too. One exhibit, *Silence, La Violence!*, let kids try to find nonviolent solutions to problems by showing them scenes of animal figures who had gotten into fights. The kids traveled back and forth among the different animals' houses to work out ways to end the disputes

KEEP IN MIND Everything in this museum is in French, including the workshops, but many staff members speak English and everything is so hands-on that kids should be able to follow what's going on without much trouble. Workshops for kids 5–12 are held on Wednesdays, Saturdays, Sundays, and holidays at 3 and daily during long school vacations. Workshops for kids 3–5 are held on Wednesdays and during school holidays at 11. (Five-year-olds can choose either.) If you have kids who want to attend a workshop and others who don't, you can head off to the Jardin d'Acclimatation (see #44) with one group while the others stay behind.

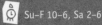
peacefully. Another show, *La Magie de Magritte,* focused on one artist's unusual imagery; kids played around with the idea of how people's faces are represented, seeing themselves in trick mirrors and hiding behind cut-out figures from famous Magritte paintings. Other inventive exhibits have taken kids on a tour through a certain period of art history or encouraged youngsters to think about concepts like citizenship.

Along with the exhibits, the museum organizes special classes for kids of all ages in which they can do all sorts of things, from painting pictures and creating sculpture to putting together machines or putting on a show. Kids visit the special exhibition and then work in groups to create something based on what they've just seen. There's even a special baby-atelier workshop for kids 3–5. This place is museum as playtime, and it's been entertaining kids and teaching them things since 1975.

HEY, KIDS! Do you have a birthday coming up? If so, bring along at least nine other kids and celebrate here. You get to play games with the museum's staff, explore the exhibits, make yourselves up, and eat some birthday cake. *Bonne anniversaire!*

EATS FOR KIDS There are several dining possibilities in the Jardin d'Acclimatation, or if it's a nice day, have a picnic in the Bois de Boulogne (see #44 and #63). One great spot is the Pré Catalan, in the center of the bois, which has kids' play equipment. If you have little kids in tow, you'll need a car or a bike to get here, however, as it's a long walk. Organic picnic goodies are available at **Les Nouveaux Robinsons** (14 rue des Graviers, Neuilly-sur-Seine, tel. 01–47–47–92–80), a supermarket/food co-op near the Pont-de-Neuilly métro stop.

MUSÉE GRÉVIN

Want to see Michael Jackson stand absolutely still? You can at this museum, because he's made out of wax, and so are a lot of other people you may or may not recognize. There's something slightly creepy about wax museums, with their eerily lifelike figures frozen in place as though under a magic spell, but everyone usually has fun picking out people they know. And this wax museum, created in 1882, has the added bonus of providing a very vivid tour through French history.

You'll see King François I meeting England's King Henry VIII in 1520, Louis XIV at a sumptuous party at the Château de Versailles, Marie-Antoinette in her cell in the Concièrgerie prison, Napoléon drinking tea with Josephine, and the French revolutionary leader Jean-Paul Marat murdered in his bathtub. (By the way, the bathtub here really is the one Marat died in; this is one tableau that's not for little kids.) Other sections focus on movie stars and on movers and shakers past and present, who are displayed in elaborately decorated tableaux complete with background sounds.

HEY, KIDS!
The world's most famous wax museum is Madame Tussaud's, which was opened in London in 1802 by a Frenchwoman. Madame Tussaud learned the tricks of her trade in Paris during the French revolution by making wax death masks of people who'd been guillotined. Creepy.

EATS FOR KIDS
Homesick? Bite the bullet and head to the **Hard Rock Cafe** (14 bd. Montmartre, tel. 01–53–24–60–00). Where else can you chow down on a good burger, fajitas, or a "Love Me Tender" kids' meal (fried chicken fillets) while staring at Michael Jackson's pants? Jugglers, singers, and who knows what else may be on hand to entertain you. Earplugs are advised for parents. At **American Dream** (21 rue Daunou, tel. 01–42–60–99–89), you can fill up on a burger or a U.S.-style brunch in a huge space filled with '50s movie memorabilia; kids are very welcome. See also Opéra Garnier.

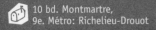
10 bd. Montmartre,
9e. Métro: Richelieu-Drouot

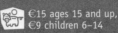
€15 ages 15 and up,
€9 children 6–14

Daily 1–7; during school holidays 10–7

01-47-70-85-05; www.grevin.com

7 and up

As for the contemporary personalities, fame is fleeting and so are these figures. They come and go depending on whether the people they represent are in the news; it's a formula that's attracted over 45 million visitors to the museum since it opened. Kids are bound to spot some familiar faces, like new residents Harrison Ford, Julia Roberts, Bruce Willis, and Ray Charles.

Kids usually like having their pictures taken while standing next to their favorite celebrities. Another hit is the Palais des Mirages, a sound-and-light extravaganza created for the 1900 World's Fair that's still wowing audiences. Its 20th-century counterpart, the Passage à Images, focuses on the thin line between illusion and reality—which is what this museum is all about.

KEEP IN MIND Has the historical exhibit here whetted your appetite for more history? At the nearby Paris-Story movie theater (11 bis rue Scribe, tel. 01–42–66–62–06, www.paris-story.com), you can see a 45-minute film on the 2,000-year-plus history of Paris in several different languages, including English (thanks to headphones). Kids can soak up some facts about Paris while sitting in a comfortable, air-conditioned space. Shown every hour on the hour, it's a good bet for a rainy day. The cost is €8 adults and €5 children 6–18.

MUSÉE NATIONAL DES ARTS
D'AFRIQUE ET D'OCÉANIE

The various names this museum has had since it was built for an exhibition on France's colonies in 1931 reflect the country's evolving attitude toward the lands it once governed. First it was called the Museum of the Colonies, then the Museum of Overseas France, and now the National Museum of Arts from Africa and the South Pacific. Sometime in 2004, give or take a few years, this museum will close and its collection will move to a major new museum on Paris's quai Branly, to be called the Musée National des Arts d'Afrique, d'Asie, d'Océanie, et des Amériques. More indigenous art from the Americas will be added to the collection, and the issue of French colonialism will be dropped completely. By whatever name, the current museum's exhibits of unusual art from Africa and elsewhere—and especially its giant aquarium, one of Europe's biggest—are bound to appeal to kids.

The museum's collection includes many very rare and beautiful pieces that show the talents of people throughout Africa and the French-speaking South Pacific as well as French-speaking countries in the Caribbean, along with a recently acquired collection of Aboriginal art from

HEY, KIDS! Know the differences between crocodiles and alligators? Crocs are longer (up to 20 feet), have a pointier snout, and have a gap in their upper jaw where the fourth tooth in their lower jaw fits. In the southern United States, alligators are much more common than crocodiles, though limited numbers of one species (*Crocodylus acutus*) are found in South Florida. (Neither species lives in France.) Crocodiles are the more aggressive creature, often attacking large animals and people. They can live a century and have remained virtually unchanged for 200 million years, proof that, scary as they are, they're doing something right.

293 av. Daumesnil,
12e. Métro: Porte Dorée

01-43-46-51-61;
www.musee-afriqueoceanie.fr

 €4.50 adults 26 and up,
€3 adults 18-25; some
special exhibits extra

 M and W-Su 10-5

6 and up

Australia. You'll see intricately carved statues and masks, stunning costumes worn by tribal chiefs on ceremonial occasions, more humble items meant for everyday use, and a huge assortment of unusual musical instruments. Ask at the desk for a copy of the "Livret Parcours," a brochure (in French) that leads kids on a kind of treasure hunt through the collection.

The basement is the site of the museum's aquarium, parts of which date from 1931, when the museum opened. It's the home of a large family of turtles; flamboyantly colored, exotic fish native to Africa and the South Pacific; and, most exciting of all, a ferocious band of huge, snapping crocodiles. Why a big aquarium in a museum devoted to African, Asian, and Caribbean arts? When the museum was opened, organizers thought it would be a good idea to display the native flora and fauna of the French colonies. Today, it's sure to be the part of the museum kids remember best.

KEEP IN MIND
The museum regularly organizes two-hour classes (in French) for kids 6 and older, with or without their parents, to teach them about the collection through games, stories, and other activities. Examples include decorating paper plates with Aboriginal designs and making up faces Polynesian-style (tel. 01-44-74-85-01).

EATS FOR KIDS At several simple cafés in the Porte Dorée area, near the museum, you can lunch on an omelet, a *croque monsieur* (grilled ham-and-cheese sandwich), and *citron pressée* (fresh lemonade). Several food shops nearby will sell you the makings for a picnic in the nearby Bois de Vincennes. **Les Zygomates** (7 rue de Capri, tel. 01-40-19-93-04) is a friendly bistro with inventive cooking and a reasonable fixed-price lunch menu on weekdays. If all else fails, head to **McDonald's** (145 bis av. Daumesnil, tel. 01-53-02-40-40). See also Bois de Vincennes.

MUSÉE NATIONAL DU MOYEN ÂGE

Travel with your kids back to the Middle Ages and have a close encounter with a mythical beast at this kid-friendly Left Bank museum. In a medieval mansion that once belonged to the Cluny abbots, the National Museum of the Middle Ages contains a rich collection of art and artifacts, but its most famous treasure is *La dame à la licorne* (The Lady and the Unicorn), a series of six 15th-century tapestries that depict strange beasts and a mysterious lady.

Kids have fun trying to work out the complex symbolism of the tapestries, five of which represent the five senses; the sixth, titled *À mon seul désire* (To My Only Desire), has provoked debate for centuries. Even younger kids should enjoy the six tapestries' exotic plants and animals, particularly the adorable unicorn, who, in the *La vue* (Sight) tapestry, smiles at itself in a mirror while its front feet rest on the lady's lap. Other items in the collection that should appeal to kids are medieval weapons and armor, a model of the Gallo-Roman baths next to the museum, and a number of objects that evoke daily life in the Middle Ages, such as a child's sandal from the 14th or 15th century.

HEY, KIDS!

The mythical unicorn, from the Latin words for *single* and *horn*, has much more than cuteness going for it. In the Middle Ages, people believed that the unicorn's horn could magically detect poisons and purify water. The unicorn was said to have the body of a horse, the beard and feet of a goat, a flowing tail, and a spiraling horn all its own.

KEEP IN MIND

Ask for the free "Comme des Images" brochure for kids when you enter the museum; even if your kids don't read French, it will help them get a handle on the imagery they will find here. The museum schedules guided tours for kids or for kids and their families (tours in English are often available), as well as crafts workshops for kids (in French) in which they learn techniques of medieval manuscript decoration, architecture, garden design, and metal-working. It also hosts concerts of medieval music, storytellers who recount medieval legends, and other initiatives that bring the Middle Ages to life.

6 pl. Paul-Painlevé, 5e. Métro: Cluny

 Sept–May, €5.50 adults 26 and up, €4 ages €18–25; June–Aug, €6.70 adults 26 and up, €5.20 ages 18–25; children 17 and under free

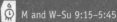 M and W–Su 9:15–5:45

01–53–73–78–00; www.musee-moyenage.fr, www.culture.fr/cluny

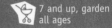 7 and up, garden all ages

Outside the museum, along the boulevard St-Michel, you can check out the vestiges of the Gallo-Roman baths on which the museum stands; they date from the time of Marcus Aurelius, the 2nd century AD. Youngsters will prefer the museum's recently redesigned garden, where vegetables and flowers typical of gardens in the Middle Ages have been planted in fanciful patterns. Little kids can even take a ride on a unicorn, a monkey, and other beasts that have found their way to an outdoor kids' play area, while older kids might want to explore the garden's medicinal simples section, with the nine key plants used in medieval medicine.

You can visit the museum's garden without touring the museum. It's a public garden with several benches, great for resting tired feet in a peaceful setting while you check out walls that date from the 1st to the 15th centuries. And it's all right here in the heart of Paris.

EATS FOR KIDS **La Crêperie de Cluny** (20 rue de la Harpe, tel. 01–43–26–08–38) serves a wide choice of main-dish and dessert crêpes. **Fish** (69 rue de Seine, tel. 01–43–54–34–69) will please seafood lovers; the friendly American owner is also the proprietor of the excellent La Dernière Goutte wine shop nearby. **Au Coin des Gourmets** (5 rue Dante, 01–43–26–12–92) prepares authentic Vietnamese, Cambodian, and Laotian dishes. In a hurry? Fast-food restaurants abound on the boulevard St-Michel. See also Cathédrale de Notre-Dame-de-Paris and Jardin du Luxembourg.

MUSÉE PICASSO

Devoted to the 20th-century's most famous artist, this museum fills a palatial 17th-century mansion in the heart of the Marais district. A real effort has been made to get kids enthusiastic about the art displayed here through guided art-appreciation tours and films and classes (in French). During the tours, given on Sundays, kids take a good look at an artwork, ask questions about it, and discuss it with a very competent staff member (parents are allowed to tag along). Even if your children can't participate in these activities, they should enjoy the art in the collection. Among the thousands of works by Picasso are 200 paintings, sculptures, and ceramics and over 3,000 drawings and prints. The museum also displays Picasso's personal art collection, which includes works by Derain, Cézanne, Modigliani, Renoir, Rousseau, Braque, and other 20th-century greats whom he admired.

Children often seem to respond better to contemporary art than adults do. They accept it on its own terms, and, in the case of Picasso, respond to his playfulness. Kids of all

EATS FOR KIDS The museum's in-house **tearoom** offers quiches, soup, salads, and afternoon tea. **Brocco** (180 rue du Temple, tel. 01–42–72–19–81) is a pastry shop and tearoom with gooey pastries and an elaborately painted 1889 ceiling. **Finkelsztajn** (27 rue des Rosiers, tel. 01–42–72–78–91), a bakery, sells high-quality take-out snacks, including bagels, poppy-seed pastries, rich cheesecake, and eggplant dip. See also Centre National d'Art et de Culture Georges Pompidou, Musée de la Curiosité et de la Magie, and Place des Vosges and the Marais.

ages wander through the galleries here, picking out works they like. Some prefer the "pink period," others the "blue period," but most are impressed by the huge *Têtes monumentales* (*Monumental Heads*) in the sculpture gallery. After viewing the collection, take a break in the museum's lovely garden or pick out an art poster in the gift shop.

In case your children ask, the building's name, Hôtel Salé, means "salted townhouse," which came from the fact that its original owner, Aubert de Fontenay, made his fortune by being the sole collector of a French tax on salt. There's a certain poetic justice in this, because after Picasso's death his heirs gave his private collection to the French government in lieu of paying inheritance taxes, and the government in turn created this museum to house the collection. Any way you look at it, it's a museum that taxes built.

HEY, KIDS! Pablo Picasso (1881–1973) was born in Málaga, Spain, where his great artistic talent was recognized very early. The first public showing of his works was held when he was just 16. After a visit to Paris three years later, he moved to France and stayed.

KEEP IN MIND Nearby, another small museum in a mansion, the Musée Carnavalet (23 rue de Sevigné, tel. 01–42–72–21–13; closed Monday), is dedicated to the history of Paris. Kids like the fantastically detailed scale models of some of the city's houses and neighborhoods as they were in the past, and a model of a guillotine carved out of bone by French prisoners of war. The museum offers lots of organized activities for children, including the Paris en Jeux class, which takes children on a tour of the Marais district in the form of a game (in French).

MUSÉE RODIN

The elegant 18th-century Hôtel Biron, Rodin's home for the last decade of his life, contains many of the sculptor's best-known works, including *Les bourgeois de Calais* (*The Burghers of Calais*) and *Le penseur* (*The Thinker*). Several of the sculptures are displayed in the 5-plus-acre garden surrounding the house, which has beautifully planted flower beds, trees, a sandbox, and lots of benches. You'll usually find Parisian parents reading quietly here, while their babies doze and their older kids run around and play. Rodin's massive yet fluid and lifelike sculptures form a calming background in this peaceful scene.

If you thought of Rodin as a struggling artist working in a tiny garret, think again; his mansion is an elegant white stone building with tall windows overlooking the garden. Within, you find some of Rodin's smaller sculptures as well as drawings and art from his personal collection—including works by Monet, Van Gogh, Camille Claudel, and other artists Rodin knew—all displayed in the mansion's large, high-ceilinged rooms.

KEEP IN MIND Recent kids' workshop themes have included portraits in sculpture, hands that speak, feelings expressed in stone, and the creation of city monuments. This small museum is definitely committed to helping kids perceive art in new ways. It's no wonder Parisian parents love bringing their kids here.

EATS FOR KIDS The Rodin Museum's reasonably priced in-house **café** has tables in the garden (open April–September). Tiny, budget-priced **Chez Germaine** (30 rue Pierre-Leroux, tel. 01–42–73–28–34) serves classic bistro dishes like stewed lentils with roast pork and, for dessert, yummy cherry *clafoutis* (a cross between pudding and a pancake). **Than** (42 rue des Sts-Pères, tel. 01–45–48–36–97) has good *nem* (Vietnamese egg rolls) and other Vietnamese specialties at bargain prices. **Le Coffee Saint-German** (5 rue Perronet, tel. 01–40–49–08–08) is *the* place for burgers, brownies, and a yummy U.S.-style weekend brunch.

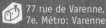 77 rue de Varenne,
7e. Métro: Varenne

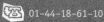 01–44–18–61–10

Museum and garden, €5 adults 18 and up, Su free; garden only, €2 adults; kid's tour and class, €4.60

 Museum June–Aug, daily 9:30–5:45; Sept–May, daily 9:30–4:45; garden June–Aug, daily 9:30–6:45; Sept–May, daily 9:30–5

All ages

Although younger kids usually prefer the museum's garden (where they can run around) to its interior (where they need to be sedate and well behaved), older kids enjoy seeing the varied works of art and maybe even trying a little sculpting themselves. Every Wednesday afternoon from 2:30 to 4:30 and several times a week during school holidays, the museum organizes combined tours and art classes for kids: one session for children 6–10, another for youths 11–15. (While your kids are busy in their classes, you can take a tour of the museum's collection yourself.) Following a guided tour of the collection (in French), children are encouraged to have a close encounter with one of the museum's artworks and then to try their hands at sculpting in wax, clay, or plaster, expressing a particular theme. They can even take their finished piece with them. (Bring a shoe box to take it home safely, as well as an apron or smock to protect clothes.) Though sessions are in French, even non-French-speakers should be able to enjoy these popular hands-on lessons, but reserve well in advance.

HEY, KIDS! The great sculptor Rodin trained to be a mason and then, after visiting a few museums, got interested in sculpture. After a trip to Italy in 1875, he began an early work, *L'Age de bronze* (*The Bronze Age*), displayed in the museum. At this point his artistic career could have ground to a halt, because the sculpture cost him a great deal of time and money, and people attacked it because they thought it was overly realistic rather than smoothly idealized. Rodin had the last word, though. His natural, realistic style eventually caught on, and he became one of the world's most famous artists.

MUSÉE VIVANT DU CHEVAL

Once upon a time (in 1719), a French prince, Louis-Henri de Bourbon, prince de Condé, had a vision: when he died, he would be reborn—as a horse. The prince, who was very rich, decided to build a horse château worthy of a princely stallion. He asked the most famous architect of the time to create Les Grandes Écuries (The Great Stables) facing his own fabulous Château de Chantilly, in the middle of a huge forest north of Paris. The prince died, perhaps becoming one of the 300 or so horses that lived in Les Grandes Écuries throughout the 18th century. Here they were visited by the likes of King Louis XV.

Today, Les Grandes Écuries is still the home of pampered horses, as well as of the Musée Vivant du Cheval (Living Museum of the Horse), which welcomes around 200,000 visitors a year. Kids like seeing the stable complex, which looks from the outside like an elegant château. Inside, around 30 well-groomed horses swish their tails in their luxurious boxes in a huge hall with a vaulted stone ceiling. All sorts of objects relating to horses over the ages fill the museum's more than 30 exhibit rooms.

KEEP IN MIND Equestrian shows take place on the first Sunday of the month at 3:30 and at other times throughout the year. The special kids-oriented Christmas show, *Noël, le cheval et l'enfant,* is one of the Paris area's best attractions for kids during the holiday season. Reservations are advised (€17 ages 13 and up, €16 children 4–12). The Château de Chantilly contains the Musée du Condé (tel. 03–44–62–62–62), which has an excellent art collection, but it's not oriented to kids at all.

Château de Chantilly, Chantilly

 €8 ages 18 and up,
€6.50 youths 13–17,
€5.50 children 4–12

03–44–57–13–13;
www.musee-vivant-du-cheval.fr

 Apr–Oct, M and W–F 10:30–5:30, Sa–Su
10:30–6 (May–Aug, also open T); Nov–Mar,
M and W–F 2–5, Sa–Su 10:30–5:30

3 and up

The main attractions, however, are the equestrian shows performed regularly in the museum's elegant *manège* (ring). Shows are based on an easy-to-follow story or theme. You sit very near the beautiful horses, who, along with their riders, wear elaborate costumes. An orchestra plays in the background. Every year in December, special Christmas shows for kids are given, in which Santa (riding a horse or donkey) encounters trouble delivering his gifts. Various characters, all of whom perform spectacular acts on horseback, help him.

The great Le Nôtre designed the elegant park that surrounds the château and stables. Kids can run off energy as parents admire the park's fountains and flowers, and in summer the whole family can take a ride on the Aérophile hot-air balloon, which is tethered to the ground but rises almost 150 meters (500 feet) above the park.

EATS FOR KIDS
In the museum, **Le Carrousel Gourmand** (weekends only in winter) has a children's menu. **Touche Nature** (22 rue de Connétable, tel. 03–44–57–02–25), a family-friendly bistro, serves organic foods. *Crème Chantilly* (whipped cream) tops cookies sold at stands around town in summer.

GETTING HERE Several trains per day run from the Gare du Nord to Chantilly–Les Gouviers. The trip takes 30 minutes, but you will have about a 20-minute walk from the train station in Chantilly to the museum. Taxis are another option from the station, although you might have to wait in a long line. If you go by car from Paris, take the A1 highway from the Porte de la Chapelle, on the northern edge of Paris, and head north to the Survilliers–Chantilly exit. Signs in the center of Chantilly point you to the Musée Vivant du Cheval.

MUSÉUM NATIONAL D'HISTOIRE NATURELLE

France's natural-history museum is actually several museums in the Jardin des Plantes, each focusing on a different aspect of natural history. The showcase collection is the state-of-the-art Grande Galerie de l'Évolution (Grand Gallery of Evolution) with its stunning parade of life-size models of African animals—giraffes, elephants, zebras, and much, much more—in the main hall.

Using the latest bells and whistles, such as interactive touch screens and games, this gallery makes natural history exciting and fun. Displays showing animal habitats come with light shows and sounds to bring the habitats alive. In the gallery's upper level, models of extinct creatures include the dodo, and a skeleton of a blue whale hangs from the ceiling, too. You have plenty of room to move around the huge, modern, perfectly lit space.

If your taste runs to mysterious specimens amassed by intrepid French naturalists, you'll be fascinated by the quirky Galerie de Paléontologie et d'Anatomie Comparée (Paleontology

KEEP IN MIND To beat the crowds in the popular Grande Galerie d'Évolution, avoid a weekend visit. Some of the pickled items in the Galerie de Paléobotanique may be too macabre for very young children (or their parents).

HEY, KIDS! Whales are full of surprises. They look like fish, but they're not. They're mammals that suckle their young the way humans do. The blue whale whose skeleton hangs over your head in the evolution gallery is the biggest mammal the world has ever known. As for the narwhal, it has a 6-foot-long, coiled ivory tusk, which makes it look like a unicorn in arctic waters. Humans have hunted whales for centuries for their meat, their oil, their bones, and the ivory tusk of the narwhal.

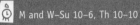

and Comparative Anatomy Gallery). When you walk in, you might want to walk right back out again, because an enormous mass of skeletons—hippos, giraffes, elephants—seems to be marching straight at you, along with a man wearing a fig leaf but no skin (so you can see his skeleton, too). There's even a room with skeletons of a dinosaur and mammoth. This museum also has a collection of creepy oddities, many gathered by 19th-century naturalists, including pickled monkeys, pickled human brains, a pickled Cyclops cat (no kidding), and skeletons of Siamese twins, all proving that Mother Nature is not always kind.

The Galerie de Minéralogie (Mineralogy Gallery) displays a stunning collection of gemstones and rocks; the Galerie de Paléobotanique (Paleobotany Gallery) features fossils and petrified wood, including a 33-million-year-old petrified fern; and the Galerie d'Entomologie (Entomology Gallery) presents 1,500 rare bug specimens. It's an amazing collection of things natural.

EATS FOR KIDS Have lunch with a giraffe, an elephant, and skeletons in the Grande Galerie d'Évolution's spacious, ultramodern **cafeteria,** overlooking the main gallery. You'll also find **snack stands** in the Jardin des Plantes. **Les Quatre et Une Saveurs** (72 rue Cardinal-Lemoine, tel. 01–43–26–80–80) prepares many vegetarian dishes using organic ingredients. **Croq' 'O Pain** (30 rue Geoffrey-St-Hilaire, tel. 01–43–31–24–80), near the museum's entrance, serves sandwiches, crêpes, and salads. See also Jardin des Plantes and Jardin de Sculpture en Plein Air.

NATURE ET DÉCOUVERTES

Want to learn how to identify trees by touch or go bird-watching in a Paris park with a guide? You and your family can do just these things thanks to Nature et Découvertes (Nature and Discovery), a national chain of stores that French kids and parents love. All the stores organize free workshops and almost-free family outings designed to teach people about environmental issues in a fun way.

The Carrousel du Louvre store gives one-hour kids' workshops every Wednesday. Children spend an hour with an instructor doing creative activities with specific themes. Learning to identify different types of leaves and making plaster casts of animal tracks are just some of the many possibilities. Classes are given in French, but most instructors speak English and can provide some translation help. If you have younger kids in tow, you and they can have fun looking at the hundreds of Earth-friendly items in the store while older

KEEP IN MIND Pick up the "Programme des Animations Pédagogiques" brochure, which lists upcoming workshops and outings. You're supposed to reserve and pay in advance (in the store, by phone, or on the Internet) for the longer outings, and it's a good idea to reserve for the workshops, since space is limited. For outings, you provide your own transportation. Other Paris Nature et Découvertes locations are in the Forum des Halles (105 rue Rambuteau, 1er, tel. 01–40–28–42–16), an underground mall; in the Palais de la Découverte (see #16); in Bercy Village (see #64); and elsewhere.

Carrousel du Louvre mall,
99 rue de Rivoli, 1er. Métro: Louvre

01-47-03-47-43;
www.natureetdecouvertes.fr

 Workshops free;
outings €6 ages
12 and up, some
outings extra

 Store daily 10–8, workshops W
varying hrs

 Store all ages, workshops
and outings 8 and up

siblings attend the workshop. The store stocks a wide range of unusual toys (some of which are always available for kids to try out), gadgets, books, CDs, and outdoor gear, and there's always a kid-oriented video being screened.

Family outings (also for anyone 8 and over) are for members of the Nature et Découvertes Club, which you can join for free at any of the stores. These outings take place outside the store and last about 90 minutes, sometimes longer. You and a small group led by a well-informed guide might go bird-watching or check out plant and animal life in a Paris-area forest. The outings provide the whole family with a great introduction to Paris's environmental issues, not to mention an introduction to French people with similar interests.

EATS FOR KIDS
The Carrousel du Louvre's **Universal Resto** (tel. 01–47–03–96–58) contains many food outlets representing cuisines from around the world; there's bound to be something to please everyone in your group. For aboveground choices, see Musée du Louvre and Jardins du Palais-Royal.

HEY, KIDS! Some items in the Nature et Découvertes stores have fastenings made from Velcro. Did you know that Velcro is a high-tech version of burrs, those prickly things that hang on your clothes when you're playing in a field? Georges de Mestral, an inventor from the French-speaking part of Switzerland, came up with the idea for Velcro after studying how burrs attach themselves to objects. He noticed that burrs are covered with hundreds of tiny hooks. The word "Velcro" comes from two French words: *velours* (velvet) and *crochet* (hook).

OPÉRA GARNIER

If you want your children to see an architectural landmark that sums up everything that was Paris in the mid-19th century, the Opéra Garnier is the place to go. Dripping with gilt and covered with every possible kind of adornment, from charging horses to the heads of composers, the Opéra Garnier was considered the height of sophistication in the days when Paris was recognized as the world's cultural capital.

The best way to introduce kids to the Opéra Garnier is to bring them to a performance here. Works that appeal to younger audiences (such as *The Nutcracker* or *The Magic Flute*) are programmed all year long and are performed by some of the world's top musicians and dancers. Even the most blasé kids can't help but be impressed by all the red plush, gilt, and general overblown elegance of the opera house's interior, especially when the orchestra starts tuning up and the curtain starts to rise on what's billed as the world's biggest stage.

Even if an opera performance doesn't fit into your agenda, you can take a guided tour of the Opéra Garnier (tours in English are available) or stroll around on your own to check out the monumental marble staircase, the 11,000-square-meter (118,000-square-foot) stage, and the main auditorium's fanciful ceiling, painted by Marc Chagall in 1964. To make all this more accessible for kids, the Opéra Garnier organizes innovative 90-minute *visites-ateliers jeune publique* (tour-workshops for children) on Wednesdays (in French). The Phantom of the Opera leads kids 4–6 around and tells them stories about all the things that have happened here, while kids 6–10 work with artists to draw elements of the decor or create their own opera costumes out of cloth; kids 7–12 have a tour and then design their own pass to the opera. These classes show kids that opera isn't just for adults; it's for them, too.

KEEP IN MIND The auditorium is closed to visitors during rehearsals; ask when you buy your ticket whether it will be open the day you visit. Most rehearsals break for lunch, so you'll have better luck at midday. Reserve at least two weeks in advance for the kids' tour-workshops (tel. 01–40–01–22–63). Special *spectacles jeune publique* (performances for kids 5–13) are organized here and at the Opéra de la Bastille throughout the year. Reserve well in advance.

OYA, JEUX À JOUER

Does your family love to play cards and board games? If so, come to this games store and game-playing center, where you can find great new games that you'd probably never come across otherwise, since most aren't distributed in the United States. Oya has a collection of hundreds of games and uses the innovative store-playing center combo to make their games more interesting and accessible to the public. Instead of taking potluck and buying a game off the shelf, you get to test it first in a "try before you buy" session. The best part is, you don't ever have to buy anything. You can come just to play any of the games, designed for different age groups and numbers of players. This is a good spot to take a break on a rainy day.

Start by choosing a table (the center has several tables and can handle up to 60 game-players at a time), and ask the very friendly, English-speaking staff for suggestions of games that will best fit your group's ages and interests. A staff member will bring you

HEY, KIDS! People have played board games for thousands of years. The oldest known game is Senet, a forerunner of backgammon, played in Egypt 4,000 years ago. It was very popular—sort of the Nintendo of the pharaohs. In fact, Senet boards have been found carved on many ancient Egyptian monuments, including tombs (for something to do when the afterlife got boring?). The world's most-played board games today are said to be checkers, Go, backgammon, chess, and Mancala (played by millions of people in Africa and the Middle East). Maybe you'll find the next classic here at Oya.

25 rue de la Reine Blanche,
13e. Métro: Gobelins

 1st game €5, 2nd game €3

T–Su 2–12

01–47–07–59–59

6 and up

a game to try out and, since the instructions that come with the games are in French and German (many of the games are manufactured in Germany), can explain the rules to you in English. Staff are also ready to help if you have questions while playing. If you want to try a second game, there's a smaller extra charge.

Some games the whole family should enjoy are Métro (based on the Paris subway system), Zicke-Zacke, and Take It Easy, but your best bet is to ask the staff to recommend a game that's right for you. Of course, you're always welcome to buy a game to take home; prices range from around €9 up to €50 (very reasonable prices for Paris). Oya is a great place to meet people, and the staff can set you up with another group of players if you like. Trying to trounce each other in a game is a fun way to make new friends.

KEEP IN MIND
When it comes to asking staff for a game suggestion, be specific. Let the person know the types of games your family likes and how much experience you have in playing them. That way you're more likely to get a game that's right for you.

EATS FOR KIDS Oya sells ice cream, candy, sodas, and coffee, and the staff doesn't mind if you bring in your own sandwich. Bakeries and take-out shops are nearby. **Le Jardin des Pâtes** (33 bd. Arago, tel. 01–45–35–93–67) features pasta dishes made with organic ingredients. See also Médaillons d'Arago, Muséum National d'Histoire Naturelle, and the Catacombes.

PALAIS DE CHAILLOT

The grandiose Palais de Chaillot, created for the 1937 Paris world's fair, is surrounded by the terraced Jardins de Trocadéro park and offers great views of the Tour Eiffel across the river. Chaillot contains two museums kids enjoy: the Musée de l'Homme (Museum of Mankind) and the Musée de la Marine (Naval History Museum). (A third museum, Musée des Monuments Français, is currently being renovated; it should reopen in late 2003.)

The Musée de l'Homme traces human history through exhibits on arts, crafts, and rituals. The huge space devoted to prehistoric peoples houses an exhibit on the magnificent animal drawings made by France's own cave-dwellers. The section on crafts and rituals includes musical instruments made by people with little means but a lot of imagination. In the À la Rencontre des Amériques (Discovery of America) exhibition, check out the magnificent red porphyry statue of Quetzalcoatl (the plumed serpent), created in Mexico in the 15th century. Kids should especially appreciate the Tous Parents, Tous Differents (All the

KEEP IN MIND If your smaller children have an attack of museum overload, treat them to a ride on one of Paris's oldest and most beautiful merry-go-rounds, set up in the Trocadéro gardens just below the Palais de Chaillot. And if you have any skateboarders or rollerbladers in your crowd, bring them here to zoom along with Paris's best skaters and boarders, who strut their stuff on the Trocadéro's terraces. If you happen to be in Paris on July 14, Bastille Day, the Palais de Chaillot is the perfect place to watch the magnificent fireworks display held at the Tour Eiffel.

17 pl. du Trocadéro, 16e. Métro: Trocadéro

 Musée de l'Homme €4.55 adults 18 and up, €3 ages 17 and under; Musée de la Marine €6 adults 18 and up, €4 ages 8–17

Both museums W–M 9: 45–5:15

 Musée de l'Homme 01–44–05–72–72; www.paris-france.org. Musée de la Marine 01–53–65–69–69; www.musee-marine.fr

 6 and up

Same Family, All Different) section, where an interactive display lets them create faces from a database of 118 pairs of eyes, 66 noses, 81 mouths, and 185 hairlines.

The Musée de la Marine demonstrates France's long history as a sailing nation. Here kids should like the gilded figures that once adorned *La Réale,* a ship in Louis XIV's navy, as well as a collection of sextants and other nautical instruments from the past. Budding sailors can have a great time identifying the models of various vessels and can watch the museum's craftspeople creating and repairing other models.

Both the Musée de l'Homme and the Musée de la Marine organize children's crafts workshops (in French), and the Musée de l'Homme regularly screens documentary films suitable for kids. All in all, the venerable Palais de Chaillot still has a lot to offer kids and their families.

EATS FOR KIDS **Le Totem** (tel. 01–47–27–28–29), a café in the Musée de l'Homme, serves light lunches, afternoon pastry, and classic French cuisine in the evening. Kids like the totem poles and the great Tour Eiffel views. At **Lina's Sandwiches** (116 av. Kléber, tel. 01–47–27–28–28) you can choose your ingredients and type of bread along with salads, drinks, and yummy desserts. Eat in the tiny restaurant or picnic on a park bench in the Jardins du Trocadéro.

PALAIS DE LA DÉCOUVERTE

The sprawling Palais de la Découverte (Palace of Discovery), opened in the 1930s and now updated for the 21st century, contains kid-pleasing hands-on displays illustrating scientific principles. As part of the museum's mission to reach out to young visitors, staff members perform around 40 scientific experiments every day that kids can watch. The "Programme du Jour" sign just inside the entrance to the museum tells you which experiments are scheduled the day you visit.

Among the exhibits, one allows you to make lightning, another to whirl the planets around the sun, another to view the effects of static electricity on your own hair, and still another to make a visual display of sounds using an oscilloscope. The École de Rats (Rats' School) is a fascinating demonstration of how animals learn. Acoustics, electromagnetic fields, spectrography, genetics, the workings of a color television, and biochemistry are

EATS FOR KIDS Affordable eateries in this high-priced neighborhood include three child-friendly chains: **Hippopotamus** (42 av. de Champs-Élysées, tel. 01–53–83–94–50), **Bistro Romain** (26 av. de Champs-Élysées, tel. 01–53–75–17–84), and **McDonald's** (140 av. de Champs-Élysées, tel. 01–53–77–21–00). Kids love **Planet Hollywood** (78 av. de Champs-Élysées, tel. 01–53–83–78–27) for its burgers, barbecue, hot-fudge sundaes, coloring books, and wild movie-land decor. The **Chicago Pizza Pie Factory** (5 rue de Berri, tel. 01–45–62–50–23) serves deep-dish pizza and has a special kids-only lunch (weekends 1–2) at the bar, complete with clowns and magicians.

Av. Franklin-Roosevelt,
8e. Métro: Franklin Roosevelt

 01-56-43-20-20;
www.palais-decouverte.fr

€5.60 adults 18 and up,
€3.65 children 5–17; family
ticket, two adults and two
kids, €12.20; planetarium
€2 ages 5 and up

 T–Sa 9:30–6, Su 10–7

3 and up

among the subjects made accessible—and fun—by the museum's creative exhibits. Kids also gravitate to Cybermetropole, a vast space devoted to the Internet, and the Planète Terre room, which focuses on the environment.

The planetarium, which has a 15-meter-high (50-foot) ceiling and seats 200, deserves a visit for its celestial show illustrating the movements of stars and planets. Even kids who don't understand the accompanying French narration can pick out familiar constellations and watch the solar system in action. The museum's popular gallery dedicated to space exploration, sure to please science-fiction-lovers, displays a gift to the museum from the United States: a fragment of moon rock brought back by the *Apollo 11* crew in 1969. Like the museum, it's the essence of discovery.

KEEP IN MIND
The Palais de la Découverte organizes classes for kids (in French) and some of Paris's most exciting special exhibitions, always designed with kids in mind. Check local events listings for details on what's happening when you visit.

HEY, KIDS! One thing you'll learn in the planetarium is that the names of constellations can be very different in French and English. For example, in France, the Big Dipper and the Little Dipper are called La Grande Ourse and La Petite Ourse, meaning the Great Bear and the Little Bear (from their Latin names: Ursa Major and Ursa Minor). On the other hand, Orion, the legendary Greek hunter and giant who found his way to the heavens, is called Orion in both languages.

PARC ANDRÉ CITROËN

This vast park covering 14 hectares (about 35 acres) on the banks of the Seine has come full circle. In the early 19th century, the village of Javel stood here, surrounded by a big, grassy pasture known for its wildflowers. The street near the park that's now called rue des Cévennes used to be called rue des Marguerites (Daisy Street). As Paris became more and more industrialized, a big bleach factory was built on part of the pasture (bleach in France is still called *eau de Javel*), and car-maker André Citroën constructed a gigantic automobile assembly plant on what remained of the open space. Both factories were eventually torn down to make way for this park, and today it offers many attractions for kids.

Now that the open space has been restored, kids can run on the grass and explore a series of gardens with different themes: the Jardin Blanc (White Garden), which has

HEY, KIDS!

It's hard to believe today, but archaeologists have discovered fossil evidence that proves that the rue St-Charles, one of the busy streets that runs along the edge of this park, crosses a trail used thousands of years ago by woolly mammoths and rhinoceroses.

KEEP IN MIND Be prepared for some begging from your children. The park's Fortis Balloon (tel. 01–44–26–20–00; www.volenballon.com) is billed as the world's biggest hot-air balloon. Tethered to the ground, it doesn't go anywhere except up and down, but the ride is still exciting, taking you over 135 meters (450 feet) above the park. Rides are given daily every 15 minutes from 9:30 to dusk, depending on the weather. Note that if you visit this park on a hot summer day, take a tip from Parisian parents and come equipped with bathing suits. Your kids will inevitably get soaked to the skin playing in the fountains; that's what's fun about this place.

Bordered by quai André Citroën, rue St-Charles, rue Balard, 15e. Métro: Javel

 Free

01–45–58–35–40; www.paris-france.org

 June–Aug, Su–T 8:30–8:30, W–Sa 8:30 AM–9:30 PM; Sept–May, Su–T 8:30–6:30, W–Sa 8:30–7

All ages

all white flowers; the Jardin Noir (Black Garden), containing all dark flowers; the Jardin des Métamorphoses, with plants that are supposed to evoke the colors of seven metals (heavy metal goes green?); the Jardin des Roches (Rock Garden), which kids can climb on; and, in a gesture to the area's past, a garden dedicated to wildflowers. There's also a labyrinth that kids love to lose you in, as well as two greenhouses.

This park's biggest attraction for kids, though, is without a doubt the fountains near the Jardin Noir. Run on computer-controlled timers, they gush forth in unpredictable ways. Best of all, children are allowed to run around in the fountains, making this an ideal spot to bring your kids on a hot summer day. All year long, however, they can work off steam on the climbing equipment, swings, and slides in the play area next to the Jardin Blanc.

EATS FOR KIDS **Le Bistro d'André** (232 rue St-Charles, tel. 01–45–57–89–14), an old-fashioned restaurant, specializes in classic dishes—like roast leg of lamb with scalloped potatoes—at very reasonable prices. At **Al Wady** (153 rue de Lourmel, tel. 01–45–58–57–18), one of Paris's best Lebanese restaurants, order a big plate of *mezze* (appetizers) and you'll please everyone. **Au Cochon Rose** (137 rue St-Charles, tel. 01–45–78–03–68) stocks picnic goodies. **Pâtisserie Lecoq** (120 rue St-Charles, tel. 01–45–77–72–56) offers temptations like the Arcachon, filled with chocolate mousse. See also Aquaboulevard.

PARC ASTÉRIX

At this French equivalent of Disneyland in a huge forest north of Paris, Astérix and his band of jovial Gauls (from a hugely popular and oft-translated comic-book series) replace Mickey and his crew. Throughout the park, actors stage performances that almost bring French history to life—though the focus is on fun rather than historical accuracy—and leave kids with a vivid impression of a bunch of rambunctious Gauls making life miserable for the invading Romans. Action-loving kids find outstanding rides they won't soon forget.

Six themed areas make up the park: the village of the Gauls, ancient Rome, ancient Greece, the Middle Ages, the 17th century, and modern times. In the first two, actors perform scenes starring the comic-strip characters every French kid knows: little, clever Astérix (the Gauls' hero); powerful, fat, gluttonous Obélix (whose job is hauling *menhirs,* huge stones the Gauls considered magic) and his dog Idée-Fixe; Panoramix, the Gauls' clever Druid; Assurancetourix, the local (bad) poet; and Abraracourcix, the Gauls' leader, fearless except when he thinks the sky is going to fall on his head. Stroll through the 17th century, and you're bound to

GETTING HERE By car, take the A1 highway north from Paris to the Parc Astérix exit. The trip is around 35 kilometers (22 miles) and takes about 45 minutes, depending on traffic. By rail, take the RER commuter train, line B, to Charles-de-Gaulle airport, terminal 1, from which you can take a Courriers Ile-de-France bus to the park entrance. Signs in the airport indicate where the bus stop is. Buses leave every 30 minutes. A combination Parc Astérix–transportation pass, sold at most métro and RER stations, covers transport and park admission. Note that park opening dates may vary; confirm in advance.

Near the village of Plailly

 €30 ages 12 and up,
€22 children 3–11

In general, Apr–June, M–F 10–6,
Sa–Su 9:30–8; July–Aug, daily 10–7;
Sept–Oct, Wed, Sa–Su 10–6

 03–36–68–30–10;
www.parcasterix.com

3 and up

see d'Artagnan and the other Musketeers in a wild sword fight.

Rides suit all tastes and ages, from an old-fashioned merry-go-round to one of Europe's tallest, scariest roller coasters, the Tonnerre de Zeus (Zeus's Thunder), and the Race de Hourra, a giant slide. Other top picks are the National 7, where kids can drive models of antique cars, and a walk through the Forêt des Druides (Druids' Forest), where giant trees turn out to be super-high slides and Druids perform creepy experiments. Youngsters can join a parade led by Astérix and his men or ride the Serpentin, a low-key roller coaster. The whole family should like the performing dolphins at the Théâtre de Poséidon and the magic shows at the Théâtre de Panoramix. On hot summer days, ride the Menhir Express (with a 13-meter/43-foot swoop) or the less-scary Descente du Styx (Descent of the River Styx) roller coasters; you're guaranteed to get satisfyingly drenched.

EATS FOR KIDS

The park is filled with 40 different snack bars and restaurants, such as **Fastfoodus** and **Selfservix** (you get the idea). At the **Cirque** (circus) eatery, you can sample Obélix's favorite: wild boar (in pâté). Several picnic areas are another option.

HEY, KIDS! Obélix—the one with the big stomach—is so strong that his job is hauling around huge stones that weigh at least a ton. How did he get so powerful? When Obélix was a little boy, the Druid Panoramix concocted a magic potion to make the Gauls strong before a fight with the Romans, and Obélix—who never says no to anything to eat or drink—drank too much of it. Now Panoramix won't let him have any more potion, so he has to be satisfied with his next-favorite treat: roasted wild boar.

PARC DE LA VILLETTE

A park for the new century, this huge park replaced decaying warehouses and slaughterhouses. There are few formal flower gardens here and few lawns you can't walk on. Instead, you find huge expanses of grass for running, curving sidewalks (good for rollerblading), bike trails, little bridges crossing a canal, and wonderful gardens and play areas designed to spark kids' imaginations.

The most exciting garden for most children, the Jardin de Dragon (Dragon Garden), contains an enormous dragon-shape climbing structure that you can descend via stairs or a long, long, long curving slide. In the Jardin des Miroirs (Garden of Mirrors), mirrors reflect magically into a densely planted band of trees. The Jardin des Frayeurs Enfantines (Garden of Things that Scare Kids) won't scare kids at all, although its strange deep-jungle noises are fun to hear in the middle of such a big city. The Jardin des Vents et des Dunes (Garden of Wind and Dunes) has a series of weird humps and mounds that children are supposed to climb on while trying to keep their balance, along with air mattresses, kites, big pieces of

HEY, KIDS!
Want to see the world's biggest bike? It's a giant sculpture of a bike by artist Claes Oldenburg, and it's displayed (half buried, actually) here in the park. It will never win the Tour de France, though.

EATS FOR KIDS Some of the 30 bright-red information centers within the park contain **snack bars**; look for the knife-and-fork symbol on park maps. Outside the park and next to the MK2 movie theater (which sometimes shows U.S. films in English with French subtitles), trendy **Le Rendez-Vous des Quais** (10 quai de la Seine, tel. 01–40–37–02–81) has a big outdoor terrace (with heaters in winter) overlooking the river and a big, noisy dining room inside. It's not too expensive if you order carefully, and there's a Sunday brunch as well as a fixed-price-meal-plus-movie menu in the evenings. See also Cité des Sciences et de l'Industrie and Cité des Enfants.

Main entrance: Place de la Porte de Pantin,
19e. Métro: Porte-de-Pantin

 Free

Daily 24 hrs

 01-40-03-75-00 or 01-40-03-75-03;
www.lavillette.com

All ages

stretched canvas that flap in the wind like sails, and other surprising stuff designed to demonstrate the effects of wind and terrain. In the Jardin des Voltiges (Balancing-Act Garden), kids can try the climbing walls and maintaining their balance on swirling disks. The Jardin des Iles (Island Garden) contains echoes of Asia, its long, narrow body of water surrounded by black-and-white rounded stones; youngsters probably won't want to linger long here, given the attractiveness of the other gardens.

The Espace Chapiteau du Parc de la Villette (at the avenue Jean-Jaurès entrance) is a big-top circus where some of the world's most innovative troupes perform. Concerts, theatrical events, guided tours, and classes for kids in gardening, architecture and more are organized in the park year-round (tel. 01-40-03-75-64 for information on classes). If you happen to get lost in this vast park, several bright-red information centers have well-trained staff ready to help. The Parc de La Villette is definitely family-friendly.

KEEP IN MIND For information on the park's current cultural events for kids and families, call or stop by the Folie Information desk at the park entrance facing the Porte-de-Pantin métro stop; it's open daily 10–7 (tel. 01-40-03-75-75). The Festival du Cinema de Plein Air (tel. 01-40-03-76-92) is a series of free open-air movies shown on a giant screen in the park (July–August, around 10 PM). You can rent lawn chairs and blankets or BYOB (bring your own blanket). Some films suitable for kids are always programmed.

PARC FLORAL DE PARIS

Created in 1969 with families in mind, the Parc Floral de Paris (Paris Flower Park) is an outstanding success. Near the Château de Vincennes within the Bois de Vincennes, it gives parents a great place to stroll around looking at lovely flowers and gives kids hundreds of activities designed just for them.

The park includes a large pine grove, a grove of oak trees (meant to remind you of those 13th-century days when good King Louis dispensed justice under a huge oak near here), a number of fountains, a garden made of specially landscaped lawn, and, of course, huge banks of flowers. Within a central section of the park dubbed the Maison de Paris-Nature is the Jardin des Papillons (Butterfly Garden), where you can see hundreds of butterflies native to the Paris area but now all but extinct (open May through October). In the Pavillon d'Information (Information Area), you can view a permanent exhibit on Parisian flora and fauna (in French, but with lots of pictures). Major exhibitions are held in the Pavillon d'Exposition.

KEEP IN MIND The park is about a mile walk from the Château-de-Vincennes métro stop, so you'll probably want to take the 112 bus from here to the park entrance (cost: one métro ticket per person). Many of the climbing activities, including a large tower and tall rock-climbing wall, aren't safe for kids under six, who could fall through the tower's rope barriers or slip off the handholds on the rocks. There are plenty of options for youngsters, however, including sandboxes, small slides, and the little train. Lovely, uncrowded paths make this a great place to bring a child in a stroller.

Rte. de la Pyramide, Bois de Vincennes, 12e. Métro: Château de Vincennes

 €1.50 adults 18 and up, €.75 ages 6–17

 Mar and Oct, daily 9–6; Apr–Sept, daily 9–8; Nov–Feb, daily 9–5

01–54–95–20–20; www.parcfloraldeparis.com

All ages

For kids, the Parc Floral contains the city's largest and one of its best-kept play areas, much of it free. They can choose among towers and other structures to climb on, enormous slides, things to swing on, and even faux rock mountains meant for scrambling up. For an extra fee, you can play miniature golf on a course set up to look like Paris itself, with the city's most famous monuments in mini-versions. There's also a lovely old merry-go-round for little kids, a go-cart track, and even a little train that runs all around the park, great for when toddlers just can't take another step. A Guignol puppet theater puts on regular performances of plays, and free shows for kids, "Les Pestacles," are given in the park's Espace Concert Delta from May through September. The Théâtre Astral (tel. 01–43–71–31–10) serves as the home base of a professional theater troupe that specializes in plays for kids (in French). Best of all, this park is quiet, clean, and rarely crowded.

EATS FOR KIDS

The park's two restaurants are **Les Magnolias** (tel. 01–48–08–33–88), with good fixed-price lunches, afternoon tea, and a terrace shaded by magnolia trees, and **Le Bosquet** (tel. 01–43–98–28–78), a classy-looking but budget-priced cafeteria and snack bar. The Bois de Vincennes (see #62) also has **snack bars**.

HEY, KIDS! The butterfly house here has butterflies native to Paris. About 15,000 different species of butterflies exist throughout the world, all of them under threat from farming and pollution. The world's biggest butterfly lives in New Guinea and is around 3 inches long with a 10-inch wingspan. You might have seen one of the most spectacular migrating butterflies, the monarch, which can fly all the way from Mexico to Canada. How can you tell the difference between a butterfly and a moth? A butterfly rests with its wings vertical (straight up), a moth with its wings opened out.

PARC GEORGES BRASSENS

You'd never guess that this hilly collection of gardens, kids' play areas, and other attractions surrounding an artificial lake was ever anything except a public park, but two statues of bulls recall the area's former existence as the site of a slaughterhouse. Named for one of France's most popular singer-poets, this park stands out from others in Paris in that its natural elements seem less hemmed in and tamed. Instead of big expanses of gravel with carefully trimmed flower beds along the edges and *pelouse interdite* (keep off the grass) signs everywhere, you find a little river running down a hill that kids can jump over and get their feet wet in, a real vineyard whose grapes are harvested and made into wine every year, and a large expanse of grass on which you can actually sit.

Kids like sailing sailboats in the lake, climbing up the belvedere (a little tower in the lake that's reached by a bridge), and riding on the park's vintage merry-go-round. Perhaps

HEY, KIDS!

Don't miss the sculpture of a donkey in this park. It's a tradition among Paris kids to give the donkey a rub for good luck. You can also sit on him and get your parents to take your picture with him; he's used to that.

EATS FOR KIDS Ice cream and drink stands dot the park. **Pâtisserie Loquer** (25 rue des Morillons, tel. 01–45–31–57–07) sells good pastries, quiches, and other quick treats. The cafés and food shops on the rue de la Convention include a branch of the kid-pleasing **Bistro Romain** (222 rue de la Convention, tel. 01–42–50–30–35), where the kids' menu lists lasagna and burgers plus a mountain of fries, along with all the ice cream or chocolate mousse you can eat. If all else fails, there's a **McDonald's** (192 rue de la Convention, tel. 01–53–68–64–51).

the most exciting of all for kids is climbing up and down a steep, rocky cliff that looks like a real mountainside while their parents watch them from a grassy slope facing the rocks.

The park's little theater is the site of regular Guignol puppet shows, and the big collection of state-of-the-art climbing equipment includes a suspension bridge, little rooms on stilts you climb up to on ladders, and all kinds of jungle gyms. A profusion of flowers supports the park's own bees; honey is made here every year, and classes in beekeeping are given regularly.

Among its innovative attractions, the park contains a fragrant *jardin de senteurs* (garden of scents), with all the plants' names presented on tags in Braille. Parc Georges Brassens is definitely a little different from other Parisian parks.

KEEP IN MIND This park is a short walk from the Marché aux Puces de la Porte de Vanves, a small flea market held on weekends along the avenue Porte de Vanves and side streets. You'll find a lot of junk as well as—if you're lucky—some treasures, from old lace curtains to quirky French kitchen utensils and maybe even toys. Older kids tend to enjoy looking at all the stuff, at least for a while, but small children and toddlers usually get bored very quickly at this or any other Paris flea market.

PARC ZOOLOGIQUE DE PARIS

If you've seen one zoo, you've seen them all, right? Well, not exactly. Paris's main zoo, a favorite among Parisian families for more than 50 years, is one of Europe's largest. It also has its own unique feature—a 72-meter-tall (236-foot-tall) artificial mountain that was built in 1934 and can be seen long before you get inside the zoo itself. Extensively remodeled using the latest technology, the mountain has elevators inside it that let you go up to platforms to get a great view of the entire zoo as well as a close-up look at the mountain goats that scramble all over the mountain's steep surface.

The zoo's permanent residents—all 1,200 of them—include lions, tigers, giraffes, camels, zebras, kangaroos, rhinos, hippos, elephants, reptiles, birds, and more. It's the usual zoo menagerie, along with rare creatures like lemurs, dwarf hippos, Eld's deer, and—the biggest hit for many kids—giant pandas. All the animals look in great shape and live in large spaces

EATS FOR KIDS Within the zoo are snack bars, drink stands, cotton-candy vendors, and French fast-food outlets. At **Le Bistrot du Zoo** (tel. 01–43–46–56–90), in front of the giraffe cages, you can sample standard French bistro fare (reasonable fixed-price menus) while checking out the world's tallest animals. The outdoor places all share that zoo-ey smell common to zoos all over the world. If this bothers you, you might want to plan a between-meals trip here, or picnic in the nearby Bois de Vincennes (see #62) before or after your visit.

53 av. de St-Maurice,
Bois de Vincennes, 12e. Métro:
Porte Dorée

€7.62 ages 16 and up,
€4.57 children 4–16

June–Aug, daily 9–6; Sept–May,
daily 9–5:30

01-44-75-20-00

3 and up

whose boundaries have been artfully concealed by plants or disguised bars and walls, making the settings seem as natural as possible.

As you enter the zoo, a big sign points out which creatures have recently produced offspring, so you can get a look at the babies. Another sign tells you the feeding times for various animals; don't miss the food-loving giant panda's mealtimes. Kids are invited to help feed the seals and sea lions every afternoon around 4:30, a chore no kid should turn down. And don't forget to look at the lookers as well as the looked at. One of the charms of this zoo is its visitors, many of them decorous, well-dressed older Parisians who were brought to this zoo as children and now bring their equally well-dressed grandchildren here, especially on Sunday afternoons.

KEEP IN MIND
Note that the zoo gets crowded on weekends. Tired little kids (and their parents) often appreciate a ride on the miniature steam engine–powered train that runs in a circle around the edges of the zoo, providing views of some animals along the way.

HEY, KIDS! The giant panda is definitely a big eater, treated at this zoo to two meals a day. And they're some meals: milk, eggs, carrots (grated, if you don't mind), bananas, apples, salt, sugar, and a 30-pound-or-so bunch of bamboo, especially grown for the zoo in a pollution-free bamboo garden in the wild Cevennes region of southwestern France. Come to the panda cage at 9:15 or 4, and you'll see just how quickly all this can disappear. No one ever had to tell a panda to finish his lunch.

PARIS À VÉLO C'EST SYMPA

9

Touring Paris by bike can be a wonderful experience, but you have to know what you're doing. Though the city government has installed what it calls bike lanes, designated by a white drawing of a bicycle on the pavement, these are mainly just sections of lanes that riders must share with buses and cars. Since Paris drivers, ever in a hurry, sometimes practice the sport called *la chasse aux vélos* (bicycle-hunting), in which the prey is a bike that's taking up space a car would like to occupy, a bike lane shared with cars is not always safe. That said, it *is* possible to bicycle around Paris without harm, and one way to do it is with a guide.

Paris à Vélo C'est Sympa (Paris by Bike is Great), a user-friendly bike-rental and tour-guide operation, organizes three-hour guided tours of the city for groups of about 10 people (families of fewer than 10 are put together). Tours in English are available, longer or shorter tours are often organized, and you can choose from a wide range of itineraries.

EATS FOR KIDS **Le Trumilou** (84 quai de l'Hôtel de Ville, tel. 01–42–77–63–98), a budget bistro, serves some good dishes (roast lamb, poached sole, crème caramel) and some not so good (dryish roast chicken). See also Place des Vosges and the Marais, Musée de la Curiosité et de la Magie, and Rollers-et-Coquillages.

KEEP IN MIND Paris à Vélo C'est Sympa rents sturdy four- and five-speed bikes for adults and kids 8–14, bike seats for smaller kids, and bicycles built for two. Reserve in advance for both tours and bikes; there's a limited number of kids' bikes. You can also rent bikes without joining a tour (€24 for a weekend, €12.20 per day, €9.15 half-day). Other rental companies are Bike 'N Roller (38 rue Fabert, 7e, tel. 01–43–37–16–17), which also rents roller skates, and the very reliable Paris Vélo (4 rue Fer-à-Moulin, 5e, tel. 01–43–37–59–22, www.paris-velo-rent-a-bike.fr).

37 bd. Bourdon, 4e. Métro: Bastille

 Tour €19 including guide,
bike rental, and insurance;
€13 without bike rental

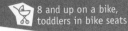 Apr–Oct, daily 9–7; Nov–Mar,
daily 9–6

01–48–87–60–01;
www.parisvelosympa.com

8 and up on a bike,
toddlers in bike seats

The "Coeur de Paris" ("Heart of Paris") trip, for example, takes you around the historic Marais district, Notre-Dame, and the Ile de la Cité, and "Paris Insolite" focuses on off-the-beaten-track sites like the architect Le Corbusier's house and the Paris Mosque. "Paris Nocturne" is a tour of the city by night, "Paris S'Eveille" takes you around the city as it's waking up for the day, and "Paris Contrastes" explores some bike-friendly spots on the city's northeastern edge, including the Parc de la Villette. Special tours for groups of young people and for riders with disabilities are also offered. Paris à Vélo organizes tours outside the city, too, such as one to the Château de Versailles. The guides are experts at leading you to out-of-the-way spots like a flower-filled courtyard around a bunch of artists' studios or a park where bikes are allowed on the sidewalks. Paris has about 5,000 streets, and this company knows exactly which ones are right for bikes.

HEY, KIDS! Did you know that the bicycle was invented in Paris in 1791? The original bicycle wouldn't win any races today, since it was very heavy and made entirely of wood. Bike-riding is very popular in France, and the world's most famous bicycle race, the Tour de France, takes place here every July. It covers most of the country (about 2,000 miles) over three weeks; American Lance Armstrong won this mega-race for the third time in 2002. If you counted all the world's bicycles, you'd find that there are around 800 million of them, outnumbering cars by almost three to one.

PARIS CANAL

To get far off the beaten tourist track while pleasing boat-loving kids, take a cruise on quiet Canal St-Martin. Head for the Parc de la Villette, on the city's northeastern edge, and hop one of the small tour boats operated by Paris Canal. From here, a leisurely three-hour cruise travels to the center of Paris through locks, a mile-long tunnel, and even a stretch of the Seine. A guide explains what you're seeing (in French and English), and you get a close-up look at a canal built in the 1820s to bring drinking water to Paris and still navigated by more than 4,000 working barges a year.

Your trip begins at the end of the Canal de l'Ourq; cruises through the wide, placid Bassin de la Villette; and then, just as kids start getting a little bored, enters the Canal St-Martin. Here you pass through the first of five big locks that take this 5-kilometer (3-mile) canal from the level of the Canal de l'Ourq to that of the Seine, your destination.

EATS FOR KIDS Hearty budget-priced dishes are the rule at the relaxed **La Chouette & Cie** (113 rue de Crimée, tel. 01–42–45–60–15). Meat-lovers go for the *magret de canard* (duck breast, prepared in various ways), and vegetarians like the wide choice of salads and other non-meat dishes. There's a special kids' play area, too. Farther away but worth the walk is **Weber Café** (Parc des Buttes Chaumont, tel. 01–42–00–45–00), in a big public park with many kids' play areas. The café serves crêpes and sandwiches all day long. See also Parc de la Villette and Musée d'Orsay.

Canal de l'Ourq, next to La Folie des Visites center, Parc de la Villette, 19e, métro Porte-de-Pantin, or Quai Anatole France, 7e, métro Solférino

€16 adults 26 and up, €12 ages 12–25, €9 children 4–11

Late Mar–mid-Nov, daily; mid-Nov–late Mar, Su only, 2:30–5:30; depart Orsay 9:30; depart La Villette 2:30

01–42–40–96–97; www.pariscanal.com

10 and up

Kids are fascinated by the locks, with their huge doors swinging open and shut and the rush of water as the boat rises or sinks. As you cruise between locks you pass through a long, narrow park, the Proménade Richard Lenoir, and under picturesque cast-iron footbridges. Near the place de la République, the boat enters a dark, mile-long tunnel eerily lit by beams of sunlight coming through air vents that reach to the streets above. You finally emerge into the Bassin d'Arsenal (near the place de la Bastille), a port where many houseboats and small yachts are docked. Then, in an exciting finale after the slow-moving canal, the boat enters the powerful Seine. You cruise past Notre-Dame and under the Pont Neuf to tie up at a dock near the Musée d'Orsay. The whole cruise is a trip back to France's past, to the days before trucks and trains, when most goods were transported on canals like the Canal St-Martin.

HEY, KIDS! The world's first locks were "flood locks" built in China in the 1st century AD. People would dam a river just upstream of rapids and then remove the dam quickly so that boats behind it would swoop over the rapids on a "flash flood" of water.

KEEP IN MIND Paris Canal also operates cruises in the other direction, from the Musée d'Orsay to the Parc de la Villette, but it's more fun to end with a cruise on the Seine. Since smaller kids may find the three-hour trip boring, this is an excursion to take with older kids who are really interested in the mechanics of boats and locks (or with babies who'll sleep the whole time). Advance reservations are required. Paris Canal also offers day-long cruises from Paris into the Marne Valley (€30, lunch not included).

PLACE DES VOSGES AND THE MARAIS

The elegant place des Vosges, surrounded by 17th-century buildings in the heart of Paris's historic Marais district, is the city's oldest square, completed in 1612 on a site where King Henri II's Hôtel des Tournelles palace once stood. Originally called the place Royale, the square was renamed to honor the first region to pay taxes to the post-revolution government. Today, the place des Vosges is a quiet little city park with many attractions for families: sandboxes for toddlers, sidewalks where kids can run around, climbing equipment, swings, and teeter-totters. The Maison de Victor Hugo (6 pl. des Vosges, tel. 01–42–72–10–16), the writer's former house and now a museum, presents a kids' story hour on Wednesdays at 2, starring Hugo's creation Quasimodo (in French).

The place des Vosges is the perfect place to begin a walking tour of the Marais, one of Paris's most beautiful districts in spite of its name, which means "marsh" (because that's

HEY, KIDS!

Rue St-Antoine was Paris's top jousting spot in the 14th–16th centuries. King Henri II was killed here in 1559 when his Scots captain-of-the-guards accidentally struck him in the eye during a match (oops). The king died in his palace; the guard was executed.

KEEP IN MIND

Quirky stores and chic boutiques abound in the Marais, one of Paris's top shopping districts. Kid-pleasers include La Charrue et Les Étoiles (19 rue des Francs-Bourgeois), for figurines from the Simpsons to Tintin; Cath'Art (13 rue Ste-Croix-de-la-Bretonnerie), for marionettes; Chat Perché (54 rue du Roi-de-Sicile), for stuffed animals and innovative wooden toys; and L'Arbre de Vie (21 rue de Sevigné), for hand-crafted toys. You'll also find lots of shops featuring oh-so-French kids' clothes, including Catamini (6 rue des Francs-Bourgeois).

Pl. des Vosges: rue de Birague and rue des Francs-Bourgeois, 4e. Métro: St-Paul

 Free

 Daily 24 hrs

 01–44–54–75–80
Mairie du 4e Arrondissement

All ages

what it was until the 13th century). Elegant townhouses (called *hôtels*), built here over the centuries by France's rich and famous, fill the Marais. Walk west on the rue des Francs-Bourgeois (lots of shops) to the rue de Sévigné; turn right and head to the square Léopold-Achille, a lovely little out-of-the-way park with well-maintained climbing equipment and sandboxes. Around the corner on the rue Payenne is another quiet park, the square Georges-Cain. Head south across the rue St-Antoine; then take the rue St-Paul, home of the Musée de la Curiosité et de la Magie (see #34); and go through one of the passageways on your right to the Jardins St-Paul, a big courtyard lined with boutiques. Kids can run around while parents window-shop. At the playground on tiny rue des Jardins-St-Paul, kids kick soccer balls against a 13th-century wall that was once part of Paris's ramparts. No one will mind if your kids join in.

EATS FOR KIDS The Marais has many tearooms and restaurants as well as food stores for picnic fixings on the rue St-Antoine. **Thanksgiving** (20 rue St-Paul, tel. 01–42–77–68–28) prepares American-style goodies to eat here or take out. **Ma Bourgogne** (19 pl. des Vosges, tel. 01–42–78–44–64) isn't cheap, but it has good *frites* (fries) and a great location. **Ay! Chihuahua** (36 bd. de la Bastille, tel. 01–46–28–63–79) serves delicious Mexican (not Tex-Mex) dishes in a big space where kids are very welcome. See also Musée de la Curiosité et de la Magie, Musée Picasso, and Paris à Vélo C'est Sympa.

PROMENADE PLANTÉE

Also called La Coulée Verte (the Green Course), the Promenade Plantée (Landscaped Trail) is a former train track that's been turned into a beautifully landscaped pathway for pedestrians, bicyclists, skateboarders, and roller skaters. It's one of Paris's top choices for a family stroll, especially since there's no traffic to worry about. The promenade stretches 4½ kilometers (almost 3 miles) from near the place de la Bastille to the edge of the Bois de Vincennes, just outside Paris's eastern limits. Sometimes it hovers high above the street, sometimes it winds through little tunnels, and sometimes it traverses hills, but park benches dot its entire length, so parents and tired toddlers can take a break.

Begin near the Bastille, where the old tracks were supported by high brick arches now called the Viaduc des Arts (av. Daumesnil). Within the arches are crafts shops and artists' studios, most with tall windows through which you can watch weavers, glassblowers, and other artisans at work. Walk up any of the stairs near these shops to reach the promenade. The walkway along this stretch is at just the right height—high enough above the traffic to

EATS FOR KIDS There's a **snack bar** along the path in the Espace Reuilly. Trendy **Le Viaduc Café** (Viaduc des Arts, 43 av. Daumesnil, tel. 01–44–74–70–70) isn't cheap, but its great Sunday brunch includes live jazz. The picturesque place d'Aligre has an open-air food market every morning except Monday—one of Paris's least expensive sources for picnic goodies. At **A la Petite Fabrique** (12 rue St-Sabin, tel. 01–48–05–82–02) you can sample 40 kinds of chocolate bars and watch them being made in an open kitchen. See also Rollers-et-Coquillages and Paris à Vélo C'est Sympa.

Entrances from pl. de la Bastille to Bois de Vin- cennes, incl. 40 av. Daumesnil, 12e. Métro: Bastille

08-20-00-75-75;
www.promenade-plantee.org

 Free

June–Sept, M–F 8 AM–9:30 PM, Sa–Su 9 AM– 9:30 PM; Oct–May, M–F 8–6, Sa–Su 9–6; some sections open 24 hrs

All ages

give you a respite from city noise, but not too high to get a good look at the people and shops below.

About halfway between the Viaduc des Arts and the Bois de Vincennes, near the Montgallet Métro stop, the walkway opens out to become the Espace Reuilly, a pleasant park with duck ponds and lush green lawns. There's also a 50-square- meter (540-square-foot) sundial on which kids like trying to tell time. The walk cuts through the middle of Paris's 12th *arrondissement,* ranked the city's greenest for the number of parks and gardens it contains, and finally ends at the Porte de St-Mandé, near the Bois de Vincennes. Strollers can stop anywhere along the way or spend a half day walking the path's full length. Older kids will have a lot more fun if they bring wheels (skates, skateboards, or a bike), especially on the promenade's eastern section, which has wider sidewalks.

HEY, KIDS! Sundi- als, yesterday's clocks, tell time not with hands but with shad- ows. A shadow is cast by a slanted object, called a "style" or "gno- mon," mounted on a dial and pointing north. It doesn't work so well at night, though.

KEEP IN MIND In spite of park guards' efforts to control the problem, some rollerbladers and cyclists in a hurry can be hazardous to pedestrians on the Proménade Plantée. Don't let your kids skate or ride their bikes too fast or guards may fine them, and watch out for speedsters if you have toddlers in tow.

ROLLERS-ET-COQUILLAGES

Le Friday Night Fever (yes, the French refer to it by this English name) has reached epidemic proportions in Paris. Every Friday night at 10 PM (if it's not raining), about 12,000 people gather on the square in front of the Gare Montparnasse for a fast-paced, three-hour, 12-to-15-mile-or-so circuit of the city—on skates. Imagine the population of a small town, all on skates, careering through the city at night, and you'll understand just how popular skating has become in Paris. If your family includes top-notch skaters, you can certainly participate in this exciting celebration of city skating, but if you'd prefer a more relaxed, family-oriented alternative, you can join the leisurely, free, three-hour Sunday-afternoon skate-ins organized by Rollers-et-Coquillages (Skates and Snail Shells), an association of skating enthusiasts.

The Sunday circuit, like the Friday one, is along a route that changes every week, is organized in advance, and is always traffic-free: the Paris police force blocks off all

HEY, KIDS!

Rollerblades are going out of style in Paris. The hot thing is "quads," skates with two rows of wheels instead of just one "blade." If that sounds familiar, it should. Until Rollerblades came along, all skates had two rows of wheels. Back to the future!

KEEP IN MIND Members of the Paris *brigade rollers* (police squad on skates) always accompany the skate-ins, and an ambulance follows just in case. Rent skates at No-mades (37 bd. Bourdon, 4e, tel. 01–44–54–07–44; reservations advised). Helmets, knee and wrist pads, and insurance are recommended. Pari Roller (tel. 01–43–36–89–81, www.pari-roller.com), a nonprofit group, organizes Friday Night Fever and coordinates information on skating in the city. Roller Squad Institute (7 rue Jean-Giorno, 13e, tel. 01–56–61–99–61, www.rsi.asso.fr) leads free skating tours for kids 12–15 on Sundays, beginning 2:45 on the Esplanade des Invalides; reservations advised.

37 bd. Bourdon, 4e. Métro: Bastille

 Free

Su 2:30–5:30, weather permitting

01–42–72–08–08;
www.rollers-coquillages.org

7 and up

roads along the routes during the skate-ins so that skaters won't have to contend with cars. Rollers-et-Coquillages has designed the Sunday event for beginning skaters, families, and anyone between the ages of 7 and 77 who'd like to visit the city on skates in a low-key way. Show up at the place de la Bastille around 2:15, and you'll usually see hundreds of skaters of all ages, some sporting very expensive outfits and high-tech Rollerblades, others in jeans with scuffed skates that have been around a very long time. Everyone is welcome, and the atmosphere is friendly and international. Rollers-et-Coquillages staff lead the way as you skate off through nearby neighborhoods. You might skate up to the Parc de la Villette and back, make a loop toward the Bois de Vincennes, or wind your way through the Marais. The pace is leisurely, and you can choose to drop out of the circuit whenever you like. But wherever you go, you'll see Paris in a unique way, under your own skate-power.

EATS FOR KIDS **Hippopotamus** (1 bd. Beaumarchais, tel. 01–44–61–90–40) is always a kid-pleaser, thanks to burgers and mounds of *frites*. **Dalloyau** (5 bd. Beaumarchais, tel. 01–48–87–89–88) is a sedate pâtisserie/tearoom. **Au Bouquet St-Paul** (85 rue St-Antoine, tel. 01–42–78–55–03) serves tasty tartines (open-face sandwiches), *tarte Tatin* (upside-down apple tart) and *frites*. Come to **The Bottle Shop** (5 rue Trousseau, tel. 01–43–14–28–04) for a generous American-style brunch on Sunday before your ride. See also Place des Vosges and the Marais, and Promenade Plantée.

SACRÉ COEUR AND MONTMARTRE

4

More postcards are sold of Sacré Coeur Basilica than of any other Paris site. As Parisian monuments go, though, this gleaming white church perched on a hill is a real newcomer, completed only in 1885. Like the Tour Eiffel and the Centre Pompidou, Sacré Coeur was reviled when Parisians first saw it, and they still refer to it as a big pastry with whipped cream on top. But no matter what you think of its looks, you should come here for the views and for a visit to lively Montmartre, a neighborhood that has much to attract kids.

Begin by taking a ride on the Funiculaire du Montmartre, a cute little funicular train that runs from the place St-Pierre straight uphill to the church. (Use métro tickets for your ride.) As for the basilica itself, kids are often bored by the dim interior, but they get a kick out of climbing up (and up and up, all 270 steps up) to the dome on the roof, where there's an impressive view of the whole city.

HEY, KIDS! There are lots of stories explaining how Montmartre got its name, but one of the most popular is that it comes from Saint Denis, who was martyred on the *mont* (butte) here by Romans in the 3rd century BC (Get it? *mont* + "martyr"). According to legend, the Romans cut off his head on a spot now marked by Montmartre's Chapelle du Martyr (Chapel of the Martyr). It's hard to keep a good saint down, though: Saint Denis is said to have picked up his head and marched north to what's now Saint Denis Basilica, which became the traditional burial place of French kings.

Sacré Coeur: 34 rue du Chevalier-de- la-Barre, 18e. Métro: Abbesses, Anvers

 Sanctuary free; dome €5 ages 6 and up

 Dome June–Sept, daily 9–7; Oct–May, daily 9–6. Basilica daily 6:45 AM– 10:30 PM

01–53–41–89–00; www.sacre-coeur-montmartre.com

 7 and up

After touring Sacré Coeur, check out the overwhelmingly touristy but colorful and kid-pleasing place du Tertre, where faux artists fill in the blanks in paint-by-number oeuvres and a few real artists may actually be plying their trade. You can hop on the Petit Train de Montmartre here, a little mock train that makes a circuit through the neighborhood while a loudspeaker broadcasts descriptions of the sights in several languages. You pass the famous Moulin Rouge cabaret, celebrated by Toulouse-Lautrec, and the Moulin de la Galette, one of Montmartre's last two windmills. The nearby Jardin Sauvage (Rue St-Vincent, tel. 01–43–28–47–63) is a little garden devoted to Paris's native plant, insect, and other animal life (yes, it still exists). The garden's enthusiastic guides, most of whom speak English, are glad to answer kids' questions. Take the time to stroll around Montmartre's tiny, steep, twisting streets to get the real flavor of this colorful *quartier*.

KEEP IN MIND
Once hangouts for artists, Montmartre's picturesque cafés were gradually replaced by porn shops and sleazy nightclubs, especially around the place Pigalle. Gentrification is now well under way, but you should still stick to well-traveled, well-lit streets if you visit Montmartre at night.

EATS FOR KIDS **L'Été en Pente Douce** (23 rue Muller, tel. 01–42–64–02–67), a friendly bistro, has inventive cuisine and a pretty terrace. Come here for lunch or afternoon tea, because at night the dining room is usually filled with cigarette smoke. The popular **La Butte Glacée** (14 rue Norvins, tel. 01–42–23–91–58) dishes up delicious ice cream. The open-air **food market** on the rue Lépic is a great picnic choice that's best on weekends. See also Halle Saint-Pierre.

SAINTE-CHAPELLE AND THE CONCIÈRGERIE

Within the sprawling Palais de Justice (Palace of Justice), now the seat of the French legal system, are two of Paris's most famous attractions, Sainte-Chapelle (Holy Chapel) and the Concièrgerie (once the apartments of the powerful royal concièrge). Both are remnants of the days when this ancient palace, then called the Palais-Royal (Royal Palace), was home to the French aristocracy, and both appeal to kids. After experiencing the sublime beauty of Sainte-Chapelle in one wing, you can stroll over to the Concièrgerie in another, to view the gloomy cells where Marie-Antoinette and other aristocrats were imprisoned before they lost their heads on the guillotine during the French revolution.

Your kids might whine "Not another church!" but they'll probably change their minds after seeing Sainte-Chapelle's wonderful stained-glass windows. This little chapel in a courtyard was built in the mid-13th century to house King Louis IX's collection of holy relics, including what he believed was Jesus' crown of thorns, which he had bought for a fortune from

HEY, KIDS!

The guillotine wasn't a bad way to go—compared to the *oubliette*, a torture chamber full of sharp knives whose name means "little thing for forgetting." Forget about it and check out the gilded clock on the Palais de Justice's northeast corner; it's been keeping time for 400 years.

EATS FOR KIDS

At **Boulangerie Cléret** (11 rue Jean-Lantier, tel. 01–42–33–82–68), friendly ladies serve breads, pastries, and light lunches to take out or eat at tiny tables. Lovely place Dauphine is a good place to find a restaurant or a park bench for a picnic. Kid-friendly **Planet Hollywood** (15 rue Arcole, tel. 01–40–51–05–44) dishes up American-style fare. Lunch with a view? **Le Toupary** (La Samaritaine department store, 23 quai du Louvre, tel. 01–40–41–29–29) has a restaurant with good fixed-price menus and a rooftop terrace café. See also Cathédrale de Notre-Dame-de-Paris and Jardin des Halles.

Palais de Justice,
4 bd. du Palais, 1er. Métro: Cité

 01-40-51-70-36;
www.paris-france.org

 Sainte-Chapelle €5.50
adults 19 and up, €3.50
children 12–18; Concièrg-
erie €5.50 adults 19 and
up, €3.50 children 12–18

Apr–Sept, daily 9:30–6:30;
Oct–Mar, daily 10–5

6 and over

the cash-short emperor of Constantinople. Sainte-Chapelle is an upstairs-downstairs chapel. You enter through a dark ground-floor chapel (with royal fleurs-de-lis everywhere) used by the king's soldiers, servants, and courtesans. The famous chapel is higher up, by way of a spiral staircase. Entering is like walking inside a rainbow. Kaleidoscopic colored light surrounds you as you "read" the Old Testament stories created in glass here by unknown artists more than seven centuries ago. Try to come on a sunny day to get the full effect.

When the royal palace was taken over and renamed during the French revolution, the Concièrgerie was turned into a prison. You can view Marie-Antoinette's cell and her initials carved in a little chapel, see a film on the Concièrgerie's past, and check out a wax museum representing the prison's most famous inmates, including Robespierre. Kids with a taste for gore can visit the Concièrgerie's Salle de Toilette, where you wouldn't want to come for a haircut: people's hair was cut off here just before their executions.

KEEP IN MIND If you have a yen to see France's legal system in action, you can visit the Palais de Justice's courtrooms (sometimes with trials in progress) and other official areas open to visitors (ages 10 and up, admission free, Monday–Friday 1:30–6, Saturday 9–1). For a special treat, come to Sainte-Chapelle for a short candlelight concert; they take place in the evenings (at 7 and 9) from mid-March to late October (tel. 01–43–54–30–09 for concert information). Near the palace, Paris's biggest flower market (pl. Louis-Lépine) becomes a bird market on Sunday mornings; kids love to wander around it.

TOUR EIFFEL

Recognized worldwide as a symbol of Paris, the Tour Eiffel (Eiffel Tower) is always a favorite among kids, maybe because it looks like something a clever kid might have designed. When the innovative 320.75-meter (1,052-foot) construction created by Gustave Eiffel began to take form in 1889, marking that year's world's fair, many Parisians—including prominent writers Alexandre Dumas and Guy de Maupassant—objected to what they viewed as a metal monstrosity they hoped would be dismantled as soon as the fair was over. Today, the tower is here to stay, and kids love climbing up and up and up endless stairs through the tower's metal frame to get a spectacular bird's-eye view of the city.

When it was completed, the Tour Eiffel was the tallest construction ever known. Even though it has now been far outdistanced by skyscrapers all over the world, including Paris's Tour Montparnasse, the Tour Eiffel still looks very, very big from the ground, where

EATS FOR KIDS **Altitude 95** (tel. 01–45–55–20–04), on the tower's first level and open for lunch only, has a very reasonably priced kids' menu (appetizer, ham, chicken, fries, dessert) along with free crayons to make pictures of the high-tech dining room. Try to reserve a table by the windows. A special elevator serves the restaurant, so you can come here without waiting in a long line. Little rue St-Dominique nearby is lined with small restaurants as well as bakeries and take-out food shops. See also Palais de Chaillot, Hôtel National des Invalides, and Les Égouts.

Champ-de-Mars, 7e. Métro: Trocadéro, Bir-Hakeim

01–44–11–23–23; www.tour-eiffel.fr

Stairs to top €3 ages 4 and up; elevator to top €9.90 ages 13 and up, €5.30 children 4–12; elevator to level 1 €6.90 ages 13 and up, €3.80 children 4–12

Jan–mid-June and Sept–Dec, daily 9 AM–11 PM; mid-June–Aug., daily 9 AM–12AM

5 and up

it stands alone in the big, flat Champ-de-Mars park. Kids are impressed by this monument before they ever get inside it, and they'll get a good look at its base if you decide to take an elevator to the top, because you're sure to spend quite some time in line. On the first level are the Cineiffel area, where a film depicting the tower's history is shown, and a display that shows how the tower is beautified with around 40 tons of paint every few years. At the gift shop and post office, you can buy postcards and get a Tour Eiffel postmark.

From the tower's top, you see the city spread out before you as if on a 3-D map, and on a clear day you can see for 50 miles. The most stunning view, though, is of the ground far below, seen through the lacy yet massive curlicues and angles of the tower's four supporting columns.

KEEP IN MIND
Around 16,000 people visit the Tour Eiffel daily. To avoid the worst of the crowds, come early or around sundown, when the light is perfect for spotting the city's monuments, or come at night when the views of the City of Light are especially magical.

HEY, KIDS! If you want to get to the top of the tower, you'll have to climb 1,710 stairs (count 'em) or take one of the elevators equipped with special brakes to cope with the varied angles of ascent. If you could put the tower on your bathroom scale, it would weigh in at about 9,000 tons. It was put together with around 2.5 million rivets and is so perfectly designed that, even in the strongest winds, it has never moved more than around 4½ inches. It can, however, become up to 6 inches taller or shorter, depending on the temperature.

UNION CENTRALE DES ARTS DÉCORATIFS

The Union Centrale des Arts Décoratifs (Decorative Arts Organization), installed in the Marsan Wing of the Louvre, contains three museums that should appeal to teens and organizes popular workshops for younger kids.

Bound to attract fashion fans, the Musée de la Mode et du Textile (Museum of Fashion and Textiles) showcases the clothes that have been in style from 1700 to today, from corsets to miniskirts. The museum's collection, only a small part of which can be displayed at any one time, contains around 16,000 outfits, 35,000 accessories, and 30,000 pieces of rare fabric. You might see the wardrobe of an 18th-century lady, creations by Yves Saint-Laurent, heavily brocaded vests worn by Parisian men during the French revolution, or the latest fashions from today's designers. It's history as reflected in fashion trends.

The Musée de la Publicité (Museum of Advertising) will eventually cover all aspects of advertising. For the moment, however, it focuses on posters, of which it owns more

HEY, KIDS!

Hear ye, hear ye! France's first poster, pasted up on Parisian walls in 1539, told people about King François I's latest declarations. Before this poster, French people got the facts from the town crier, who strolled through town yelling out the latest news.

KEEP IN MIND The Musée des Arts Décoratifs' Artdécojeunes program (tel. 01–44–55–59–25) runs two-hour workshops in French for kids 4–12, divided into groups according to age. Workshops begin with a game that takes kids through the collections, followed by a hands-on session in which children can construct something. They might make a decorative object in medieval style, design a poster, or create a fashion item out of cloth. The workshops are held on Wednesdays and school holidays. If your kids want to take a class here, reserve a month in advance. Long-term crafts classes are also given.

107 rue de Rivoli, 1er. Métro: Palais-Royal, Louvre

 €5.40 ages 18 and up, workshops €10

 T and Th–F 11–6, W 11–9, Sa–Su 10–6

01–44–55–57–50; www.ucad.fr

Museum 12 and up, workshops 4–12

than 80,000 from the 18th century to today. You can check out every kind of poster, from a playbill pasted up in Paris in 1744 to gorgeous posters designed by Toulouse-Lautrec and contemporary advertising posters. The problem is that most of these posters are visible only on computer screens; you take a virtual visit of the museum's collection, not really a kid-friendly activity.

The Musée des Arts Décoratifs (Museum of Decorative Arts) is going through complete renovation, and as of this writing, only one section, Moyen Âge–Renaissance (Middle Ages to Renaissance), is open. However, this alone is worth a visit. You walk through a series of rooms decorated just as they would have been back then, giving kids a visual representation of how some French people (the wealthy ones) actually lived. The fabulously colorful and richly decorated medieval Salle Raoul Duseigneur room shows that the so-called Dark Ages were anything but.

EATS FOR KIDS The Marché Saint Honoré contains food shops and restaurants. **Le Pain Quotidien** (18 pl. du Marché St-Honoré, tel. 01–42–96–31–70) has salads, sandwiches, and hot chocolate; little kids have trouble on the high stools. **La Ferme** (55–57 rue St-Roch, tel. 01–40–20–12–12), prepares organic sandwiches and other treats to eat in or take out; come before 1 to avoid crowds. At the Scandinavian **Nils** (36 rue Montorgueil, tel. 01–55–34–39–49), choose among salads, sandwiches, and fruit tarts. See also Musée du Louvre, Jardin des Tuileries, Jardins du Palais-Royal, and Jardin des Halles.

CLASSIC GAMES

"I SEE SOMETHING YOU DON'T SEE AND IT IS BLUE." Stuck for a way to get your youngsters to settle down in a museum? Sit them down on a bench in the middle of a room and play this vintage favorite. The leader gives just one clue—the color—and everybody guesses away.

"I'M GOING TO THE GROCERY..." The first player begins, "I'm going to the grocery and I'm going to buy... " and finishes the sentence with the name of an object, found in grocery stores, that begins with the letter "A." The second player repeats what the first player has said, and adds the name of another item that starts with "B." The third player repeats everything that has been said so far and adds something that begins with "C" and so on through the alphabet. Anyone who skips or misremembers an item is out (or decide up front that you'll give hints to all who need 'em). You can modify the theme depending on where you're going that day, as "I'm going to X and I'm going to see..."

FAMILY ARK Noah had his ark—here's your chance to build your own. It's easy: Just start naming animals and work your way through the alphabet, from antelope to zebra.

PLAY WHILE YOU WAIT

NOT THE GOOFY GAME Have one child name a category. (Some ideas: first names, last names, animals, countries, friends, feelings, foods, hot or cold things, clothing.) Then take turns naming things that fall into that category. You're out if you name something that doesn't belong in the category—or if you can't think of another item to name. When only one person remains, start again. Choose categories depending on where you're going or where you've been—historic topics if you've seen a historic sight, animal topics before or after the zoo, upside-down things if you've been to the circus, and so on. Make the game harder by choosing category items in A-B-C order.

DRUTHERS How do your kids really feel about things? Just ask. "Would you rather eat worms or hamburgers? Hamburgers or candy?" Choose serious and silly topics—and have fun!

BUILD A STORY "Once upon a time there lived..." Finish the sentence and ask the rest of your family, one at a time, to add another sentence or two. Bring a tape recorder along to record the narrative—and you can enjoy your creation again and again.

GOOD TIMES GALORE

WIGGLE & GIGGLE Give your kids a chance to stick out their tongues at you. Start by making a face, then have the next person imitate you and add a gesture of his own—snapping fingers, winking, clapping, sneezing, or the like. The next person mimics the first two and adds a third gesture, and so on.

JUNIOR OPERA During a designated period of time, have your kids sing everything they want to say.

THE QUIET GAME Need a good giggle—or a moment of calm to figure out your route? The driver sets a time limit and everybody must be silent. The last person to make a sound wins.

HIGH FIVES

BEST IN TOWN
Cathédrale de Notre-Dame-de-Paris
Cité des Enfants
Jardin du Luxembourg
Jardins du Palais-Royal
Médaillons d'Arago

BEST OUTDOORS
Jardin du Luxembourg

BEST CULTURAL ACTIVITY
Marionnettes du Luxembourg

BEST MUSEUM
Cité des Enfants

WACKIEST
France Miniature

NEW AND NOTEWORTHY
Promenade Plantée

SOMETHING FOR EVERYONE

ALL AROUND TOWN

MANY THANKS!

This book is dedicated to my daughter, Ghislaine, who makes Paris even more fascinating by helping me see it through a kid's eyes. Thank you also to my wise and wonderful editors Andrea Lehman and Linda Cabasin, without whom this book would never have been written. And a special thanks to those who have shared their expert opinions on things to do in Paris with kids: David Burke, Raphael Triolet, Elana and Jake Cohen and their parents, the staff of Oya, and Arnaud Lemoing. Finally, *un grand merci* to all the many Parisians in all walks of life who belie the city's reputation for chilliness toward foreigners by being warm, friendly, helpful, and not afraid to practice their English when necessary.

—Emily Emerson

the end.